From The Bottom Of My Heart

Experiences of a
Jamaican/Canadian doctor
on four continents

Colin E. Forbes

MD, CM (MCGILL), FRCPC

Copyright © 2016 by Colin E. Forbes

All rights reserved.

No part of this publication may be reproduced, distributed, or transmitted in any form or by any means, including photocopying, recording, or other electronic or mechanical methods, without the prior written permission of the publisher, except in the case of brief quotations embodied in critical reviews and certain other noncommercial uses permitted by copyright law.

Wholesale discounts for book orders are available through Ingram Distributors.

ISBN
978-1-988186-84-9 (softcover)
978-1-988186-85-6 (ebook)

Published in Canada.

First Edition

Table of Contents

Acknowledgments vii

Chapter One — Early days in Jamaica 1

Chapter Two — Early schooling. 11

Chapter Three — America 17

Chapter Four — Jamaican holiday 29

Chapter Five — Canada 33

Chapter Six — The Canadian Pacific Railway. 41

Chapter Seven — Medical school. 57

Chapter Eight — The Army 81

Chapter Nine — Back to the RCAMC 101

Chapter Ten — Babies 105

Chapter Eleven — West Germany 109

Chapter Twelve — England 129

Chapter Thirteen — Return to Canada. 137

Chapter Fourteen — Off to Africa 145

Chapter Fifteen — Nigeria 163

Chapter Sixteen — Back to Canada 173

Chapter Seventeen — Nairobi 177

Chapter Eighteen — International health. 181

Chapter Nineteen — Private Practice 195

Chapter Twenty — Family holidays 225

Chapter Twenty-one — Pat and Punkie 235

Chapter Twenty-two — Home on Tate Close 239

Chapter Twenty-three — Kitisuru and
                                  personal challenges. 255

Chapter Twenty-four — Final African exit. 265

Chapter Twenty-five — London, Ontario. 279

Chapter Twenty-six — Jamaican winter holiday. 301

Chapter Twenty-seven — Back to Canada 315

To my Margaret.

Acknowledgments

Some of the many friends who have
helped me with this book:

My grandaughter Kelli Forbes Smith who translated my scribble to readable type. My friends Cecil and Leona Isaacs on Walpole Island where I started to write this book. Louise Pyne, who read the first script. Helen van Houten who did the serious editing in Africa. My family Robert and Claudia Forbes and Faith and Don Drayton for their efforts in Jamaica. Dave McMillan and my critique group from London Writers Society. Pamela and Julia Forbes for their support. Ellie Walton of "Move to the write" for polishing, and to all the others whom I have left out. As we say in swahili "asanta sana" (merci).

Chapter One

EARLY DAYS IN JAMAICA

That was certainly a sore throat. I was nine years old and riding back with my family from our country home in Newport to Kingston. Since I had such a high fever and was obviously ill, my dad decided to stop at the home of the man who lived in Old Harbour on a large farm. I was given some aspirin, a warm "bush tea" and put to lie down in a room off the veranda. Just outside, the adults sat drinking their tea, nibbling cucumber sandwiches and chatting loudly enough to keep me awake. I listened intently to that conversation—it was to instill opinions in my mind that would affect my life greatly for the next ten years. Mr Court was a white Jamaican landowner farmer from a "big" family. "Big" in the Jamaican context at that time meant established, respected, powerful, rich and usually white or "near white". "Near" refers to the shade of colour of skin, texture of hair, quality of speech and similar traits.

Mr Court did most of the speaking. My father, mother and Mrs Court joined in occasionally, giving examples of personal experiences. They were all deeply religious folk. Here are some of the statements I heard: "I don't know what is happening in Jamaica. The people think that this rubbish about Independence will help them. If we break away from England can you imagine what will happen to this island? How will these cuffees rule us? They can't even speak properly and they have no respect for the white man. They tell the poor black people that they are equal to the white man—ever heard such rubbish? Bustamante and his JLP (Jamaica Labour Party) are whipping up my farm labourers—telling them they should be paid more and that when we are independent, he will be prime minister and will make sure that they will get more pay.

"On the other hand, Norman Manley is also twisting their minds. You'd think he would know better: he's from a decent family, studied law in England and is married to an English woman. He is twisting people's minds with his PNP type of communism, and they are beginning to believe him. You see how all this is affecting the people. They don't even want to call you "mista" or "missis" anymore; and they have no manners." This talk came floating in at me through the window, and I was impressed, depressed, confused and afraid.

The fear came mostly because here I was, the darkest member of my family, with unmistakable "nigger hair", thick lips and given to outbreaks of the Jamaican patois, which was barely understandable to my parents. I learned this beautiful, expressive, fun-filled language from Mattie, my nanny, cook and best friend as she spoke at length with her friends in the back yard. These friends included Phillip, the mechanic (who had served a stint as a wartime farm worker in the US—I adored him for that); Uriah, the quiet, smiling and often drunk carpenter; Baba, the single-toothed old lady who cared for us with her bush tea baths when we had chicken pox; and a host of other people who came to our back door: the vegetable seller, the fish monger, the "partner" *peakapow* (Chinese lottery) representatives. "Partner" was the forerunner of micro credit. Each member would contribute a weekly amount, then draw out the entire saving when their turn came. This system still exists in Jamaican expatriate groups in North America and in the United Kingdom, where it is the solid financial base of these communities—far more reliable than the fast-talking, thieving "financial advisers" who prey on such communities.

The Forbes Family.

So as I listened to these sentiments through the window, bad thoughts buzzed in my head. Suppose Mr Court and his family found out that I was really a nigger? Would they hurt me, would they hurt my father? He was the slightly dark one whose genes magnified themselves in me. My mother was a white-skinned, quiet, religious lady from a large family. The ten children in my mother's family demonstrated the wide racial and colour variation that centuries of intermingling produced—from her and Uncle Elmsley, indistinguishable from white, to Uncle Ken—very dark and "negroid" (as they used to say). Fortunately, we escaped from the Courts without obvious harm, except for the fear that I had experienced and that I experience occasionally to this day. I could not understand my father's role in all of this. He did subscribe to much of Mr Court's sentiments but at the same time he devoted much of his life to the care of the poor and the underprivileged (the blacks).

My father was an outstanding chartered accountant with a thriving private practice in the middle of Kingston's business district, 18 Duke Street. He was an only child in a family whose name, Alexander Forbes, belied a genuine Scottish connection. As with most Jamaican families of this time, our African connection was never sought—or even mentioned. He had an excellent education—at Wolmer's Boys School, which all three of his sons attended also. He travelled extensively, to Cuba and to Toronto. He played cricket and was a member of the Kingston Cricket Club whose grounds, Sabina Park, were familiar to me as I often sat outside the bar after the matches and saw and heard tales of the great cricketers of the day including George Headley. Dad was a devout member of St George's Anglican Church and we dutifully attended services there every Sunday. We sang the old hymns, recited the collect of the day, and slapped at mosquitoes around our ankles. Around 1942, a powerful English evangelist named Harold Wildish came to Jamaica. My father took us to hear him in a big tent and we were all "saved". Wildish was an imposing man with a compelling voice—few who heard him did not "get saved".

Being saved profoundly affected our family, as my father and mother embarked on a new form of life. Dad gave up his pipe and his regular tipple of whiskey ("rum degrades a man, whiskey uplifts him," he would say). He left the order of Masons to which he had belonged and in which he had reached elevated positions. He devoted his life to helping others find Jesus Christ as their personal saviour. I was a willing follower in his footsteps. He became well known among the ever-increasing number of North American evangelists who found Jamaica fertile ground for their missionary work, and a close winter retreat. Our home was jokingly referred to as the "Forbes Hotel" by one smiling Canadian missionary as he noshed down Mattie's rice and peas at our table.

Billy Graham.

Dad had always been a kind, helping person. On paydays, a seemingly never-ending line of men and women would come to the back door of his office to receive money to meet their tearfully outlined needs. They had to come to the back door, because his secretary or my mother were at the front office and they objected strongly to these folk "taking advantage of him". His philanthropic work—in the name of the Lord—expanded. He founded the Youth for Christ movement in Jamaica, a popular American evangelist movement that thrived under his leadership. I was deeply involved, singing in a quartet, organizing the Saturday night meetings at the Ward Theatre, giving testimony, and often preaching the sermon. We were joined by a group of young people—mostly all light-skinned Jamaicans, who threw themselves into the exciting, spiritually rewarding endeavour.

Youth for Christ was but one of my father's many outreach programs. He regularly visited the prisons, preached to the inmates and brought them gifts; he also had services on the beach for the poor and often homeless children who lived there. He founded the Gideon's in Jamaica, and the Caribbean Christian School for the Deaf. In all these endeavours, he was genuinely interested in the welfare of the poor and saw his work as uplifting for them. He certainly did not demonstrate any racial prejudices and his spiritual base was among black people. Nor did he benefit financially from his Christian work; on the contrary, he funded most of this work personally and that was later to cost us dearly. But he and I had major disagreements when it came to class.

Youth for Christ group.

Like most of his peers and friends, he was convinced of the value of class. Society was a simple structure based on class. The highest class was the white foreigner—and at the top of this pile were the English. He considered us fortunate to be ruled by such a civilized, cultured, intelligent, generous people—the basis of his objection to independence and self-government. Next on the higher rungs of the class ladder were the white Jamaicans. They represented what a locally born and bred person could achieve. They were almost all wealthy and their behaviour was always under national scrutiny. The inevitable variations in social and behavioural standards were an anomaly to be pitied rather than censored. Even their drunkenness, thieving or marital failures were either hidden or excused. The light-skinned blacks were next on the ladder. They were probably the most vociferous in condemning blacks and treating them harshly. Then there were the blacks, who made up the vast majority of the population.

At that time, most blacks willingly accepted their servile role. They accorded the utmost respect, obedience, trust and loyalty to all above them on the social ladder. Their existence depended on demonstrating these attitudes to the upper classes, who provided their wages or earnings.

Rumblings of discontent were starting among the blacks, fueling the fire between the two main political parties. Crime was starting to grow and develop. The end of the Second World War saw the return of hundreds of young men and a few women who had served overseas in the defence of England. The officers were well rewarded but the enlisted black men got little or no compensation. A few of them formed the core of an important emerging group—the Rastafarians. These men dropped out of the prevailing social structure and some went into the hills behind Kingston Harbour to live in communes where they would be away from the arm of the law. They freely smoked marijuana or *ganja*, but their main endeavor was to found and develop a new religion, Rastafarianism. It was based on the strict laws of the Old Testament and the belief that God had revealed himself through Haile Selassie, the then emperor of Ethiopia. The concept of a black man having his own kingdom was appealing to this group and the movement grew quickly. The government quickly vilified the Rastas and their easily distinguishable appearance of unshaven, unkempt hair (dreadlocks) and beard that grew to be a badge that aroused fear and mistrust in many of the population, although in fact they were overall a peaceful bunch, trying to exist outside the colonial boundaries.

Chapter Two

EARLY SCHOOLING

I attended Wolmer's Boys School—an elitist school founded some three hundred years earlier. Nearly all the staff were young Englishmen plus a few brown Jamaicans. When we did get a black Jamaican Latin teacher, he stood in front of the blackboard to introduce himself and the class wags chanted "where's he gone!" Wolmer's was certainly the important formulating force in my life. We were disciplined for any infraction of the rules. I was caned by the head for clowning in class—imitating a teacher with protruding upper incisors. The head had me bend over then gently tapped my rear with the bamboo cane, revealing the telltale sound of the exercise book padding of my bottom so I sheepishly removed it before he delivered "six of the best".

I was not an academic enthusiast. I learned only what interested me and crammed the rest for exam purposes only. I could see no point in learning the dates of various wars that the English won or the reigns of the Stuart or Tudor families. Mathematics was beyond my realm of understanding. I was fascinated by the beauty of Shakespeare's and Wordsworth's poems. The headmaster, Mr J.R. Bunting, taught them. He was an outstanding young Englishman in his twenties whose appearance, manners, speech and behaviour I was to emulate for the next decade or so. Sport was the most enjoyable pastime and stamp collecting was my hobby. I was never outstanding at sport, except tennis—which was to occupy my fun life for the next sixty years. I followed all school games—cricket and football—closely and worshipped the heroes who brought fame and glory to the school. I clearly remember riding the tram back home, victorious in a football game with Kingston College, and cheering repeatedly our school cheer "strawberry shortcake, huckleberry pie, V-I-C-T-O-R-Y, Are we in it? Well I guess, Wolmer's, Wolmer's, yes, yes, yes!" When we approached the large private hospital, Nuttall, I loudly implored all the boys to be quiet in respect for the sick and no doubt dying who lay within. When the tram became silent, a glow of self-righteousness crept over me.

I tried hard to develop my skills at tennis. My father built a court on our front lawn and we used it to improve our game. One of my father's relatives was one of the island's tennis champions. He was an officer in the army, and one night in the mess a fellow officer from England called him a nigger. My cousin then shot the Englishman in the leg and was put in jail for ten years. When he was discharged, my father gave him a job in his office, and we became good friends. He taught me a lot of tennis tricks and I often acted as a ball boy for his tournament games. He asked me once to be his doubles partner in the Liguanea Club tennis tournament. I quickly agreed but shook in my boots when I learned that we were playing against Errol Flynn and his partner. They trounced us, thanks to my bumbling service returns as I merely stood gawking at the movie idol who was my absolute hero. Errol was an aficionado of Jamaica. He sailed into Port Antonio in his yacht, the *Zaca*, and moored at Navy Island, which he bought. I understand that his wife still lives there. The word got around the usually unreliable island gossip net that he transported girls from Wolmer's Girls School to the island and gave them exciting weekends.

We travelled all over the island in a second-hand wood-framed Chevy station wagon, which we called "True Love" due to its unpredictably smooth path. I did most of the driving, usually with my current heart throb sitting squeezed between me and my father in the front seat. The frequent stick shift changes, thanks to the Jamaican roads, gave me lots of opportunity to fumble the nether regions of my beau. That was as far as I went in the sexual field. Intercourse, or the very thought of it, was anathema to us and the punishment was more than we could bear to imagine. We formed a male quartet and belted out hymns and songs of faith all over the island. I tried to harmonize but the sounds that came out were usually horribly off-key. One day, when our family was taking a long walk along the road in the cool evening of our village of Newport, we came upon a family walking towards us. They seemed to know us (everyone did) so we chatted. They were missionaries visiting from America. They then sang for us the beautiful hymn "What a Friend We Have in Jesus" in lovely close harmony. I was more impressed by that than I was by the prevailing hit parade number one—"South of the Border" by Frank Sinatra, which was heard all over the island all the time. Many years later, after much contact with missionaries from North America, my father donated our country house with most of its 130 acres of land to an American missionary group. I later heard that the house became a whore house. I visited it once and it had been completely destroyed.

Our contact with the outside world was through the local newspaper, *The Daily Gleaner,* and the shortwave radio. We listened mostly to the BBC and to the American evangelical station CJBC from Quito, Ecuador. The BBC kept us posted on the progress of the war. One Sunday afternoon, I heard the program interrupted to announce the Japanese bombing of Pearl Harbour. We were told that this was unimaginable and only evil-minded, dirty people like the Japanese would do such a thing. At least that brought the Americans into the war and many young Jamaican men were sent to the US to work as farm labourers. VE Day was announced to us as an emergency message at school by the head and we all cheered! We had been fiercely loyal to the Allied forces as we followed their progress. I was a member of the Army Cadet Corps and was genuinely interested in all things military. Names like Field Marshall Alexander, Lord

Wavell and General Montgomery struck awe in me. I was fifteen years old when the war ended—so I just escaped the sixteen-year cut off when boys could lie about their age and join up.

I had been bumbling my way through school, managing to scrape through with minimal effort. Math was my most difficult subject—one couldn't bluff through that! Latin could be crammed into one's head and spewed out at the exam—although I still remember some of the more important words and linguistic principles. In those days Latin was thought to be important in the study of medicine. This was the field that my parents had envisioned for me, and they were gently nudging me towards it. My mother once pointed out that it would be good for me to become a doctor. As I was so dark, becoming a doctor would allow me more social acceptance and respect. I could certainly see her reasoning and went along passively, but fearfully, as I also knew that one had to be bright to become a doctor and I wasn't bright, certainly not as bright as the "brains" in my class.

One of them, Edward Seaga, the son of Lebanese Jamaicans, went on to Harvard University and performed brilliantly. He developed a deep social consciousness, and on his return to Jamaica, he became deeply involved in politics. He joined the JLP and once lived in a slum area of Kingston, giving him enough acceptance to be elected as the prime minister of Jamaica. Eddie and I had been close at school, and I greatly admired his scholarship and his devotion to the plight of the poor.

I barely squeezed through my Cambridge school certificate exam, thanks mainly to the mark I got in art, a subject I had chosen as an elective. I liked drawing faces and I became particularly good at drawing my comic book heroes—Superman, Batman and the Lone Ranger. To my surprise, on my art exam I was presented with a red hibiscus flower and told to draw it—in pencil! Fearfully but resolutely I spent the next two hours replicating the beautiful flower. It got me an A and I squeaked through that certificate—which I have framed.

Chapter Three

AMERICA

After high school, I was entitled to proceed to university. There were none in Jamaica then, so my father decided that I should go to a Christian college in the USA. Friends helped him choose Taylor University in Uplands, Indiana. It was a small Methodist college with a high scholastic standard and rigid Christian principles and rules. After much preparation, buying clothes and holding a few gospel meetings, I left one morning in September 1947. The small airport in Palisades, outside of Kingston on the Port Royal Road, was packed with my family and friends, some tearful. My nanny Mattie pushed through the throng, hugged me, and gave me a piece of ginger to chew to counter the inevitable stomach problems that would develop in the air.

Mattie was closest to me of all the household memories. She was a small black lady with a ready smile and an infectious laugh. She cooked delicious meals for the extended family and unexpected friends. She also did most of the housework. My father had a joking relationship with her—calling her "Mrs Lewis"—but he never went into the kitchen. I spent much time with her in the kitchen, shelling peas, cleaning and mashing spinach, cutting the crust off the cucumber sandwiches that she made for tea—I still adore those bits! While doing this, Mattie would be chatting away—mostly warning me about some of my friends. She would warn me about some of the boys whom I invited to our house, especially those who were black and from a lower social class. "Don't let those *cuffees* come to the house, Mr D. You don't know if they will steal things." *Cuffee* was a derogatory term used for the perceived lower social classes. Mattie called me Mr D because I stuttered badly, especially over words beginning with "D". My brothers and sisters found this amusing and taunted me about it.

Mattie (centre) with Fay and Dave.

I hated being teased or mocked or laughed at. Once when my mother had one of her afternoon teas with her lady friends, I was helping Mattie to serve the cucumber sandwiches and I tripped and spilled the entire tray. The ladies were aghast. A throaty-voiced, cigarette-smoking English lady whom we called "Aunt Pansy" exclaimed "How clumsy he is!" and they all agreed. I mention this because it is an example of the kind of behaviour I fear most, and I realize that much of my own behaviour is aimed at preventing people from treating me in that way. During my kitchen time, Mattie also would be pulling my leg about my romances and expressing her concern for various members of the family. She was particularly disappointed at the way my mother treated her after Mum's religious conversion. Mum seemed to be critical of Mattie's every move, sometimes expressed in outbursts of anger. Mattie told me about them and I tried to help her through them. Mattie had one child, Cissy, for whom my father and mother showed great concern and supported in many ways. Cissy eventually went to the USA. She returned to Jamaica and lived with her mother until her death, when she inherited her mother's beautiful small house in Kingston.

I took a Pan American Airways "China Clipper" to the USA. It was a seaplane that went around in ever-increasing circles until it had enough speed to become airborne. We winged our way over Cuba and someone pointed out Guantanamo Bay—a name that I remembered well when it gained notoriety. September is the Caribbean hurricane season and we ran straight into one. The plane lurched and shuddered, and fell repeatedly. Seated across the aisle was Betty Payne, a beautiful girl from Wolmer's Girls. I saw her horror-stricken face as she said "Colin, we are surely going to die". I agreed and said appropriate prayers. Calm returned, and soon we landed in Nashville, Tennessee. There I waited in the airport to be transferred to the plane that would take me to Indianapolis.

An old black sweeper came up to me and softly warned "Son, them seats ain't for us folks—move quickly over there before you get in trouble." He pointed to an area signed "For coloureds only" and only then did I notice the sign over where I sat, "Only for whites". I quickly transferred to "my place" and that was the first lesson in my

American experience—"know your place". I sat in "my place", scared stiff that someone would have seen me in the whites-only seats and would punish me. We all knew about the power of the men in white hoods who lynched blacks who did not know their place. Fortunately I soon boarded the plane to Indianapolis and arrived safely at Taylor University.

It had imposing grey brick buildings and lovely quiet grounds a few miles away from the nearest small town—Uplands. I was welcomed with some degree of interest and curiosity. I was to be the only foreign student and the only black man in the college. I was allocated a room that I had to share. My roommate was a large, friendly white farm boy named Wendell, and he seemed to bring all the odours of the farm with him to our cramped quarters. I slept on the top bunk.

On the following day we had an opening night dinner party—a rather formal affair to introduce the freshmen. The boys were at one end of the curved staircase and the girls at the other end. As names of pairs were called out, couples were formed as someone came down each side of the staircase. The boy gracefully offered his arm to his partner and led her to the large hall. My name was called, then two girls' names. One of the girls was a very beautiful dark-skinned lass—she was an American Indian—and the other was a virtually white lass with African facial features and hair. I offered both arms and we fearfully entered the hall—obviously "out of place". My girls were afraid of me and we barely spoke all night.

Some folks asked me about Jamaica—were we still slaves of the British? How did I learn English? Where did we live? What did we eat? My room was my refuge and I spent hours at my desk writing home and crying over the photos of my family and my current girlfriend, Helen R, who promised to wait for my return to get engaged. A couple of months later I heard that she had another boyfriend—Dick McIntosh, whom she later married. My brother Ronald married her sister and they had two children before they divorced. I did notice that my window faced another wing of the building, which was obviously the girls' dorm. Occasionally, I returned to my room after practising basketball at night and flipped the light on, only to be ordered quickly to turn it off. Wendell would be seated at the window with his friends, who were announcing "second floor, third on the right" as a poor unsuspecting lass got undressed for bed. I quickly learned the code and joined the chase. Slowly I made friends with a few of the boys who were brave enough to befriend me. One of them, Hank Proffit, who had been aircrew in the war, invited me to his home in a nearby Indiana town for Thanksgiving. His family were warm and kind to me and explained at great length that they bore no ill will towards Negroes.

I was very confused because it was evident that I was being accepted solely on my status as someone who was different and historically linked to an inferior race. This concept was novel to me, as I had considered myself a member of a privileged class and worthy of acceptance as such. One day, I was chatting with a group of my "friends" when we were joined by a tall, handsome, blond-haired basketball hero. A friend was quick to introduce me and I offered a handshake. He stretched out his left hand and said "Left hand for niggers" and laughed loudly. I shook his left hand but I was deeply hurt and ashamed. Later, my friends apologized for his behaviour and explained that he was from a big family from the South.

The Indianapolis 500 was a famous car race, which I longed to see. I was told that the easiest way to get to Indianapolis was to hitchhike—"just get on the road and smile and hold your thumb out, and someone will pick you up". I got out on the road early and did just that—and gave up after about six hours. My friends explained that they forgot that I was "coloured".

Inevitably, my hair grew to the point where I needed a haircut. I walked into Uplands and went to the barbershop. The kindly looking barber got up from the chair and led me to the door saying "We don't cut Negroes' hair. Did you know that this was the town where the last Negro north of the Mason Dixon line was lynched? Just leave and don't cause no trouble son!' I left, and cried all the way back to my room.

At Easter, my friends suggested that we go to New York. We would buy a car and drive to the big city. I was eager to go and explained that I had an aunt in New York. My aunt Marie was a legendary relative of my father, and I was sure that she lived in sumptuous surroundings such as I saw in the movies. I wrote her and she agreed to house the five of us. We set off in the cramped car for the long drive. Our first stop was in Terra Haute, Indiana. We all went to the stools at the counter and started our orders; when the cook got to me he explained "We don't serve niggers here, don't cause any trouble". I quickly returned to the car. My friends brought me a hamburger and a Coke and I had a pee in the woods. When we eventually reached New York and found Aunt Marie's home it was on the third floor of a tenement building and had one bedroom, so we all slept on the couch, on chairs, and on the floor. She was deeply apologetic but she did cook us nice food.

I was overwhelmed by New York—the height of the buildings, Times Square, pretty white girls walking the streets and offering tantalizing temptations. I read the deeply moving inscription on the Statue of Liberty: "Send us your poor . . .". Our visit to Washington was moving for me. I looked at Abraham Lincoln as he sat gazing out and I could hear his voice, "We hold these truths to be self-evident, that all men are created equal . . .". Then I imagined Thomas Jefferson booming out the Bill of Rights. We saw the Liberty Bell in Philadelphia and learned about the Civil War and the abolition of slavery. I sat in the car on the long drive home and tried to match up the sentiment that I had just heard and read about with the experience I was having in America. I couldn't equate them—then or now.

The Americans reviled the British way of life that we had in Jamaica. "You keep servants? That is wrong, how can you do that? How can you obey a king and call his family names like Prince, Earl, Duke, and so forth? Why do you allow some people to be awarded with titles such as 'Sir' and 'Lord?' We don't do that in America—our government is elected by the people, for the people, of the people."

That all sounded so grandiose and self-praising but I just could not accept those boasts because of my own humiliating and terrifying experiences. The British made no attempt to conceal their class-based society. I later heard workers in Covent Garden market boast "I'm a working class man", meaning "I am from a lower class of society", usually in comparison with some middle- or upper-class person. Later in the army I was struck by the clarity that characterizes the institution—we had "officers" and "men". We wore our rank on our sleeves and a sergeant would not dare (or indeed aspire) to enter an officers' mess. I pondered on the possible virtues of applying these conditions to an entire society.

The justification for the existence and continuation of both these societal structures—the class-based British one and the classless American one—was the loudly proclaimed assertion that each treated the more deprived members of their society in a more acceptable way. "We treat them as members of our own family. We do not hate them; we like them as long as they behave or know their place. Some of our best friends are coloureds or fishmongers."

I often heard Christians defending their superior race attitudes by quoting from the Bible: "Servants, obey your masters . . ." and the many references to class and tribe divisions in the Bible. This advice was difficult for me to accept and I began to doubt my own acceptance of these anomalies in my Christian beliefs and practices. They came to a crisis once at Taylor, when we had a black Jamaican pastor speak at one of our assemblies. He was a young man who had been saved at one of our Youth for Christ meetings. He had a bright, outgoing personality and a booming "preacher's voice". His message was loud and clear—prejudice against black people was rampant in the Christian church in the USA, and that was a sin and should be stopped. These were days long before Dr Martin Luther King and such noises were unbelievably radical and totally unacceptable in the Christian society of that part of America. This message scared the daylights out of me. I saw it as unfair of him to say such things at my college, when I was begging for acceptance as a real Christian despite my African roots. I wished that my appearance was not so obviously "negroid". He had stated his wish to see me for lunch after his talk, but that was the last thing I wanted. I locked myself in the toilet and stayed there, afraid and trembling, pulling at my hair, wishing it was straight, pinching my nose to narrow it, pursing my lips to make them less thick. Later that afternoon, when I was sure that the Jamaican preacher had gone, I slipped out of the toilet, up to my bed where I remained under my blanket crying for the rest of the day and night. Fortunately, no one seemed to pay any attention to what the black man was saying. At least my small circle of friends didn't, so the next night we returned to our favourite pastime in our darkened room, watching for the bare-naked girls in the dormitory across the quadrangle.

I learned to study just hard enough to pass the exam. This included studying how to read and write an exam—a skill that I was to master over the next eight years with such success that I eventually reached my life goal of becoming a doctor. In those days, multiple-choice questions were in their infancy and most of the exams were of the essay type. "Compare and contrast", "define", "describe", "evaluate" were challenges that gave one the opportunity to waffle one's way through the paper or bullshit as the skill is sometimes appropriately called. As I approached the end of my first year, I begged my father to allow me to go home for the summer holidays. This would be a burden financially for him but it was imperative for me. I just had to regain my sanity, self-respect and confidence, all of which had been stripped from me. I got my ticket back to Jamaica, eagerly packed my suitcases and proceeded by bus to Indianapolis. I sat down to await the bus and was quickly told that coloured folk were not allowed in that hotel but there was a park outside with special benches where I could sit and wait. I quickly gathered my bags and ran to the park. Sitting down, I shook with fear and disgust at my treatment. I proclaimed aloud (but softly) that as long as I lived, I would never return to that country. I have kept that promise over the past fifty years, except for a few short visits.

In all fairness, I did have a few enjoyable experiences at Taylor, and I learned some useful lessons. Being it was just post-war (1947) we had quite a few older veterans. These men were friendly to me and I enjoyed their company. I was most impressed by their war stories. One of them, Ben, was almost completely bald, which greatly upset him. I missed him at supper for a few nights and asked about it. Sheepishly, he explained that the stairs leading to the dining hall had bright lights over the landing under which he had to wait to enter the hall. He said he was ashamed of the light shining on his head and felt that everyone was watching him and laughing at him. I assured him that this was not so, but he did not believe me. He took extra food from his lunch and ate in his room every night. He explained that his ship had been torpedoed in the Pacific and for two days he was floating until he was rescued, and that the experience had caused his hair to fall out. I admired him.

I was also introduced to American humour, which was mostly in the form of cynicism and mockery. Much of it was directed against subjects and people whom I venerated. Wine was called "Methodist fruit juice", the Lord's Prayer began "Our father who art in heaven, Harold be thy name." That most useful rhyme was converted to "30 days hath September, April, June and no wonder, all the rest have peanut brittle except Gramma Moses who has a red bicycle with yellow tyres." All of these derisions provided me with much laughter, which was good for me at the time. I had no other pleasures—I had not conversed at any length with any girl for the entire year. This was mainly because I was afraid both of being rejected by the girl and of possible repercussion from my peers.

Chapter Four

JAMAICAN HOLIDAY

Back in Jamaica, I implored my father not to send me back to America. He thought that Canada would be a better place for me. He himself had lived in Ontario for a short while and enjoyed it. He described McGill as a well-respected university in a French-speaking city. I was eager to try that out and fortunately, I was accepted into the second year of a four-year bachelor of science (pre-med) course. This was a great relief to me, despite the threat that I had to learn French. I had never taken it in high school but was proud of my Spanish, which I have never had occasion to use. Most of the holidays were spent in Youth for Christ work. I became quite an accomplished preacher, and as I was now a BTA (been to America), I was in demand. I clearly remember one weekend we went to Old Harbour, a fishing village not far from Spanish Town, the old capital of Jamaica. A tropical storm had hit and many fishing boats were caught at sea. The entire town was devastated, so we called for a prayer meeting. I did the service and we prayed for the safe return of the fishermen. I also appealed to all present to take the opportunity to give their lives to the Lord and be saved, just as we wanted their relatives to be saved at sea. We sang a very touching hymn:

> Precious Lord, take my hand,
>
> Lead me on, help me stand,
>
> I'm tired, I'm weak, I'm worn.
>
> Through the storm, through the night,
>
> Lead me on, to the light.
>
> Take my hand, Precious Lord,
>
> Lead me home.

I was emotionally overcome by the sweet harmonious singing of this and other hymns. Jamaican church singing still moves me to tears. People came streaming up to me at the altar in response to my plea for them to accept the Lord as their personal saviour. That gave me an enormous feeling of power—and I can now understand the popularity of the present-day evangelists and their strong hold over the emotions (and purses) of the thousands of their followers. Hitler would have been a good evangelist!

Much of that holiday was spent in preparing for the biggest-ever public family event—the marriage of my sister Norma, whom we all called Muffet. She was a strikingly beautiful, very light-skinned lass who attracted many suitors. She almost got betrothed to one whom my father deemed unsuitable—he was too dark. So he took her on a long trip to Canada and Europe. The Atlantic boat crossing also produced some "near miss" romantic adventures. Finally to the family's great relief, she agreed to marry Peter, a close schoolmate of mine who was blond haired and blue eyed. He was a brilliant student and as his mother was the manager of a popular spa in the country, he often stayed with us in Kingston. He had a marked stutter and strange facial involuntary movements but his superb intellect was much admired by his peers. The wedding was a big affair and strangely enough, I accompanied the couple on their honeymoon—acting as chauffeur. One of the beautiful spots we visited was Dunn's River Falls by Ocho Rios on the north coast. The river's churning white waters rush over navigable rocks into the quiet beckoning sea. We all bathed there and joyfully frolicked in the warm waters. We had been joined by one of my sisters' friends—Pam, a café-au-lait coloured girl with a shy, dimpled smile. I swam quietly up behind her and held her waist. She jumped involuntarily then melted back to me. It was obvious that I had more than a platonic or athletic interest in her, so she quickly extirpated herself from my arms and warned me not to try such tricks again. The twinkle in her eye belied her real meaning. My future advances were unsuccessful. That was perhaps the first lesson I learned in the chasing-down-the-girls game—not every woman in the world wants to be laid by me. That had a double-edged effect on me—I vowed to sharpen my skills in romanticizing and I developed a severe fear of rejection by women whom I fancied. These dilemmas remained with me for a long time.

Sharpening those skills included improving my looks and general appearance. I had earlier embarked on a course offered by Charles Atlas as advertised on the back of most comic books, as "I was a 97-pound weakling", with the photo of a very handsome man with bulging muscles. The course taught a method called dynamic tension, which was tensing one's own muscles for long periods. It certainly worked for me and I was able to emulate Mr Atlas's posture at the slightest provocation. I also started to do push-ups and I continued to do them all through my life. I did one for each year of life, but when I reached 70 I thought that was taking a joke too far, so, with the onset of spinal stenosis I stopped them. I also sought to improve my general appearance in my dress. It was important for me to look like an American. Phillip had brought back an American Air Force jacket for me and I also started to wear the flattened-down, round crown felt hat in the "pork pie" style, which was to be my trademark for the next few years. I left for McGill, hoping and praying that I would have an easier time in Canada than I had had in the USA.

Chapter Five

CANADA

I arrived in Montreal on a blustery September autumn day and proudly displayed my acceptance papers to the Bachelor of Science pre-med course. I was briskly told to wait outside for the Boulais bus to take me to Dawson College in Saint Jean d'Iberville. The facility was an ex–Royal Canadian Air Force base to which were sent the male Bachelor of Science students, mostly vets, plus all engineering students. It was a desolate place outside of Montreal consisting of a collection of rounded buildings—quonset huts—surrounding larger hangar-like structures. I was allocated a small room in B8, not far from the main gate. It was bare but comfortable with a squeaky bed and a small desk. The common washroom and showers were at the other end of the halls. It was anything but the ivy-covered, imposing buildings shown on the McGill folder. There were 14 rooms and most of us occupying them were foreigners. Pete from the USA was next to me and Carlos from Cuba was across the hall. Spyros the Greek was at the end of the hall and we became good friends. I was told that my entrance into second year was dependent on my passing a mathematics course—calculus. This was my weakest subject and I tried desperately to understand it as I knew that my entire future depended on my passing that exam. Spyros promised to get me through the exam if I would teach him English. He explained that I didn't really have to understand calculus, just learn a few formulas and spit them out at the exam. I did this and I passed—and to this day I have no idea what calculus is all about. I did my part, and Spyros speaks grammatically excellent although heavily accented English.

Dawson College had a character of its own. We were isolated, unsupervised and longing for fun. The winter came and we were snowed in. I followed the gang to the gym at night to play basketball. I never could get the ball into the basket. I put my jacket on and ran briskly through the snow tunnel to my hut. One night I saw a large crowd lining the snow-sided path and I was told to wait if I had $2.00 and see what would happen. Soon a short, round lad came running absolutely naked through the snow over to one of the huts. He disappeared then returned with shoes and a large coat on to collect $2.00 from each of us bewildered onlookers. When I asked why did he do it, I was told that he was a Jew and "Jews would do anything for money". Anti-Semitism was rife at McGill at the time and my Jewish pre-med friend explained that he had to excel in his studies as there was a quota for Jews getting into medical school.

I studied hard; there was little else to do. At about 10:00 pm one night I noted a general exodus to the main gate. I found a small wagon with steam pouring from it and a French-speaking couple all bundled up in the sub-zero weather expertly preparing and selling hot dogs—*chien chaud*. I quickly learned to order mine with *moutarde*, and ask for *vinegre* for the *patate frites*. Once while returning to B8 with my hot dog *moutarde* dripping on my chin, I looked up and saw an incredible sight in the sky. It was a series of dancing, ever-changing coloured lights. It was the aurora borealis—the northern lights—a moving experience of the beauty of God's universe.

We rarely ventured into Montreal so when the Winter Fair came it was a real treat. We saw the exquisitely carved ice sculptures done by the various fraternity houses. There was also the crowning of the McGill Ice Queen. Only one female lived at Dawson, a homely lass who was brave enough to enter Engineering. Dawson decided to enter her into the Ice Queen competition. We voted en masse for her and she won. The main campus beauty queens had to split the votes amongst themselves. There was considerable correspondence in the *McGill News* about this—"unfair" they called it, but we were very proud of Doris and she was now the campus kitten, not the ugly duckling. Dawson had few or no moral standards. The college cheer that we loudly proclaimed at basketball and floor hockey games was:

Dawson one, Dawson twice,

Bim bam, God damn,
Ooooooooh shit!

There was a Singer sewing machine factory nearby, and we had regular dances to which the girls from the factory would be bussed in. They were as eager for companionship as were we students, so there was much bed creaking after the dance. I never attended these dances because at the time I did not drink alcohol and I was fearful of women, especially those who spoke no English. My formerly religious attitudes and beliefs were fraying at the edges. I did not attend church and barely prayed. I was happy in my newfound freedom and excited to find that there was fun outside church. I passed my second-year exams (including calculus) and again went home for the summer—the last time for the next four years. My family found me a changed man. I was less inhibited and developing a "social consciousness". I challenged the class and colour beliefs of my society and family and spouted a neo-communist line. Fidel Castro had established himself in next-door Cuba and dealt harshly with the rich white and near-white rulers of the island—he was anathema to my family and our friends. They feared that his teachings might spread to Jamaica and destroy us—which they effectively did.

One afternoon I was discussing my theories about the injustice of Jamaican middle upper-class society to the poor, and my father got very upset—we were shouting, probably for the first time. He accused me of becoming a communist and quoted Biblical verses about "servants, obey your masters", and the parable of the faithful servant. That was the first time we had an outright verbal battle, and it upset us both. His philanthropy was now threatening his personal finances and I know that it was difficult for him to continue paying all the expenses for my education.

So on my return to McGill—this time to the main campus in Montreal—I tried my best to minimize the amount of my father's contribution. I heard of an opening at a Christian society boarding house—Student House of the Intervarsity Christian Fellowship. It was in the middle of Montreal on Peel Street, adjacent to McGill. There was an opening for a janitor at the student residence and I eagerly applied for it. Mostly on the basis of my professed evangelical Christian faith, I got it. This meant that I got free room and board in exchange for janitorial duties such as cleaning the common areas and the bathrooms and toilets, setting the tables, serving the meals and washing the dishes for 36 people three times a day, and keeping the entrance free of snow. I immersed myself in this job.

There were many social and religious functions at Student House and I was again deeply involved in Christian affairs. Despite my background I was not really admitted to the inner circle of the super-evangelical group. The first winter, I went with the group to a ski resort in Morin Heights. It was a simple, comfortable lodge with a huge fireplace. I tried to ski but failed miserably so I spent my time by the fireplace. Once I was joined by a blonde-haired, pretty, shy lass from Peru who explained that she did not like skiing either. She seemed interested in me so we chatted amicably until I felt that it would be safe to take her hand, with the excuse that my hands were cold (they were burning hot). Just then Bill—the student Christian leader—came in and found us so I quickly let go. He later explained that this behaviour was unacceptable and I must never repeat it. I apologized profusely.

A group from the house, led by Bill, regularly went to the evening service at the Westmount Baptist Church. The pastor was a charismatic silver-haired man who was a riveting preacher—we nicknamed him Rev. Shakespeare. Walking home, the group paired up into couples, except me of course, who dragged behind. Bill then came by my side and confidentially explained that he understood just how lonely I must feel. He told me there was another church nearby that was a Negro church and maybe I would be more comfortable being among "my own people". That was a great revelation to me, as I honestly thought that the folks at Student House were "my own people".

So the next few years were again lonely ones, but all my energies were concentrated on two things—getting through pre-med so that I could become a doctor, and finding money to pay for this education. For the latter, I became a seasoned hustler. I cleaned homes—entire large Westmount homes—for an entire weekend for $5.00. The work included scraping the floors with steel wool, polishing the oven, cleaning the fridge, and so forth. One kind lady, as she paid me the money on her return from a party on Sunday night, said in her gin-soaked voice "You have done such a wonderful job, I wish I would pay you more." So did I! I also got a job at a Wonder Bra factory, packing and shipping at nights. I became an expert at sizing bras and practised guessing the sizes that various women wore. I suppose that this was a factor in what would become my lifelong interest in the female breast—from one point of view (pun not intended) or another. We were a motley crew at this factory night shift, mostly McGill or Sir George William College students. Beside me on the packing line was a tall, handsome coloured man who I later learned was a PhD student at the theological college. We became friends and shared our experiences with racism in ecclesiastical places.

Chapter Six

THE CANADIAN PACIFIC RAILWAY

My big break came at the end of my third year. I was hunting for a summer job and after several unsuccessful attempts I was told by a West Indian classmate, "Why don't you just give up trying to get those jobs like a waiter in Banff, clerk in an office, and so forth. Those are for white boys only. Just come and join us on the railway." So I eagerly went to Windsor Station and applied for and got the job as a sleeping car porter on the Canadian Pacific Railway. That was exciting as it opened a new door for me. It provided me with an education that was different from but certainly as valuable as that which I was to obtain in my pre-med years at McGill. The summer intake of porters was university students, all of African descent, but varying in colour and nationality. Most of us were from McGill or Sir George William College but we had a few from the American universities for blacks, such as Meharry, Tennessee State, Howard and Fisk. It was these students who were to provide me with information on race relations in America—from the black standpoint.

We were all issued with uniforms: smart serge grey trousers with black stripes on the side and a few spotless white starched jackets with high round collars. The hat was a pill-box, carried in a green cloth tie bag, and a shiny brass sign proclaimed "sleeping car porter". I proudly possess mine to this day, and use it as the take-off point for my porter stories at dinner parties. We quickly learned to walk the porter walk with all these clothes slung over our shoulder. Porter walks were of three types. One was the going-out walk—upright, brisk with a slight skip-hop movement on alternate steps. Another was the coming-home walk—a slower, more tired version of the first with a distinct limp to signal our physical distress, maybe accompanied by a slight groan and "my dawgs are killing me", as we waited for sympathy. The third was in the train as it sped on, lurching from side to side as we took sharp bends on the track or gentle turns. We maintained a broad-based gait leaning our body in opposite direction of the curve. To do this without holding on to the seats as we wrote down orders for drinks or wake-up times was a sign of an accomplished, expert porter. It took some practice but I mastered it eventually, and proudly demonstrated it at every possible occasion. I also use this to demonstrate in my dinner party presentations these days. The only problem is that I perform mostly after a few drinks and I don't always straighten out on completion of the Rocky Mountain curve walk.

The new intake of porters had to go through a proper porter school. Our headmaster was an elegant, tall, slender, greying gentleman called "Doc" Weaver. He was an American and rumour had it he had been a medical student from Meharry who once came to work in his summer holidays but never returned. I was admonished by an old porter, "Son, you are a good porter and you seem to enjoy it. Don't be stupid like Doc Weaver. Go back to school and finish your medical studies and be a doctor. Don't spend the rest of your life as a god damned porter." The words rang in my head through the bad times ahead.

Doc's first duty was to cleanse us—he lined us up against the wall and frisked us. He recovered a couple of flick knives from our American colleagues. "You don't need these," he explained. "You are going to get Whitey's money the other way—by working your arse off and jiving him dry." "Jiving" was a code word for playing the role you thought the customer wanted, such as smiling (showing teeth), singing—"Ole Man River" was the favourite— even doing a few dance steps, hence the descriptive term. He explained that we would make money by using our head, our teeth, and our hands and feet. Heart was not a vital organ in this endeavour and truth was not mandatory. We learned the tricks of the trade—practical, emotional, honourable, professional. Some of the practical things we learned were how to place the metal box step and help the passengers onto and down from the car, how to make up the bed for sleeping with the double fold of the sheet at the bottom for easier placement of the toe or foot, how to swing a pillow into a pillowcase and how not to fiddle with it tucked under the chin while opening the case.

Emotionally, we learned that all long-distance travellers have a story to tell so we could be helpful if we just listened to them every now and then. Honour and respect were to be gained from the passengers and were reciprocal. Doc warned us all, "Don't ever fuck around with white women on the CPR—that's the quickest way to hell." He explained that we could never get away with it and we wouldn't enjoy it anyhow—too much commotion in a confined space. The professional aspect was strange to me. He regarded portering as an honourable profession and he did not want us to bring dishonour to it. Such things as stealing, violence, sexual misdemeanors, forgetting the disembarkation point of a passenger or failure to protect an elderly passenger were inexcusable.

We completed our porter school and were ready to start. In the summers, most of our passengers were long-distance ones, often the parents of war brides from the UK who had settled on the West Coast. They travelled the cheapest way, which at that time (1949–50) was a "hotbox"—a non-air-conditioned car pulled by a steam engine. Unpopular with the regular porters, they were usually manned by the "summer boys". I took several of these cars across Canada, sometimes starting at Halifax and ending five days later, at Vancouver. These were fascinating journeys. The route was awe-inspiring—through the large cities of Montreal, Toronto, Winnipeg, Calgary and Vancouver, to the wilds of north Lake Superior with its rocks and bashing waves, to the long straight stretch of the prairies, to the wonders of the Rockies.

I quickly realized that I would gain extra marks by giving passengers a running commentary on the route, so

I bought all the handbooks that would enable me to do this. In my best porter voice I would explain as we clickety-clicked over the prairies, "This is the longest stretch of railway line in the world" and, "We are now travelling at 120 miles per hour."

"Oh my" they would gasp.

Or, "That is Mount Eisenhower and over there are the Seven Sisters. Now we're leaving Field and we shall descend 200 feet into Nelson. During the descent we shall go through the Figure-of-Eight Tunnel—one of the engineering marvels of the world. Construction was started at either end and they met in the middle—right?" These sights were as exciting for me as for the passengers and I gained great respect for the wonderful folks who planned and constructed this railway line and opened up this beautiful country. Our work was extremely difficult. The car was uncomfortable and extremely hot. We had to open up the windows, which let in soot from the engine. Soon we were all covered in it. As one dear old Scottish lady observed, "Porter, we all look like you now!"

At one station in northern Ontario, a whistle-blow stop, I once dutifully opened the door and placed my step-down. Quickly I was grabbed from behind by my fellow porter and the door was closed. "Don't you know this is the black fly capital of the world—we'll all get bitten to death, asshole."

The carriage held thirty-two bed spaces—eight on each side and eight upstairs. That meant every evening I had to prepare thirty-two sleeping spaces. The sheets were starched and I had to open them, spread and fold them in the prescribed way, and cover them with the blanket.

Then I had to fold up the upper bunks until they were ready to be occupied. In the morning, when everyone was at breakfast in the dining car, the process was reversed and the sheets collected in the dirty linen bags for storage.

Sleep was a luxury. We were officially allowed two to three hours per night. At this time we could climb into our allotted upper bunk and try to get some rest if not sleep. The cars all had a bell station from where emergencies could be located and dealt with. On our sleeping shift, we were allowed to hook up our bell station to the next car whose porter was then supposed to be awake. If your next car was manned by a regular (old) porter this rarely happened. Rather, on completion of their own evening tasks, they would hook up to your car and head off to bed. This meant that often one would have little or no sleep for five nights!

The first time I took a transcontinental car over, I arrived in Vancouver and after a lengthy closing down process, I wearily piled into the porters' bus and was delivered across town to the porters' quarters. I was soon to be familiar with these places in many cities across Canada and some in the US. They were in the seedier parts of town where the black folks lived. We were housed in a huge dormitory-style room with beds on each side and large tables in the middle. Here I would flop exhausted on my bed and prepare for a well-earned sleep marathon. I watched the old porters shirtless with their suspenders covering their undershirts and cigars dangling from their lips. They seemed energized and took out bottles of whiskey as they sat down at the table to start their marathon poker game.

On an early trip, one of them, a kindly old gentleman, came to my bed and explained, "Look son, I know you're tired. I know that you have a lot of money from tips. You must be careful because they'se lots of thieves here. Take your sock, put all the money in it, tie it around your wrist and then go to sleep." I followed his instructions and woke up 13 hours later. My sock dangled from my wrist empty, with the end cut off. The card game was still in progress and the emotional and decibel levels were high.

I was devastated! In a strange city with absolutely no money and a three-day layover until I returned to Montreal. I showered in the communal bathroom and dressed in my "civvies". Fortunately, I found a $5 bill forgotten in my shirt. I went around the corner for coffee and toast and tried to plan my next move. I realized that it would be best to stay away from the quarters as much as possible. Fortunately, I had my tennis racket with me, so I went across Vancouver to the public tennis courts at Stanley Park. I strolled around watching the players when a young man asked me, "Want a game? I'm John". I explained that I only had a racket but no tennis gear. He quickly produced shoes from the clubhouse and we had a fun game. He then asked me if I wanted to go to his home for lunch. I tried to disguise my eagerness but I don't think I succeeded. I was soon in what seemed to be a palatial mansion being served a sumptuous lunch by his charming, kind mother.

Three days and several tennis games and delightful meals later, it was time for me to return to Montreal. This time, I was to "dead head"—travel back without having a sleeping car to service, basically to spend the entire four-day journey goofing off. I travelled in the caboose during the day. The caboose was the last car on the train, usually inhabited by the conductor and a few off-duty staff. The conductor invited me to help myself to coffee. The train was a long one with mostly empty freight and passenger cars. It went very quickly through the circuitous track in the Rockies. As I poured my coffee, the inevitable happened—it spilled over some important-looking papers. The conductor took a slow languid suck on his pipe, drawled a common railway man epithet and said, "Don't do that again, son". I was relieved at the tone of his admonition. He was a kind man, and he asked me if I had ever seen a cowboy rodeo. I told him that I had only seen it in movies. "You gotta see the stampede," he ordered. "Get sick in Calgary."

When we arrived there I reported to the station master, He looked at the pitiful sight I presented and wrote out a three-day sick pass to remain in Calgary. He handed it to me with a wry smile. John had given me $20 so I guarded it with my life. I went to a nearby restaurant for dinner and was served the stampede special steak. It was a huge slab of meat served on the large wooden slab. It took me quite awhile to demolish it.

The show started the following morning. I got up early for the parade down the main street. It started with the sight I had dreamed about for much of my life—a single file of red Indians in full feather head-dress and regalia, riding beautiful spirited horses, bareback. They took about one hour to pass. I looked at the faces of these men, old and young, and a few women with children mounted in front of them. I shall never forget the look on those faces—all I dreamed about from the movies. The expression is best described as "resolute". I thought I saw anger, boredom, disgust all overridden with pride and a hint of superiority. I saw no smiles. Then came the fun with ox carts, daredevil riders, covered wagons. There were no chain-store or coffeehouse advertisements—at the fairground it was pure fun. Wild cowboys lassoing wild horses or riding ferocious bulls. I thoroughly enjoyed myself and I felt so privileged to witness a sight that I had dreamed about ever since I saw Tom Mix movies. You can only imagine just how confused and disappointed I was to hear white and "foreign" Canadians speak about indigenous Indians in a derogatory way, blaming them for spoiling the cities like Vancouver with their drunkenness on the street and evident pockets of poverty in the beautiful city. "They've taken enough of our tax money, they have been given more than enough land, seen one totem pole you've seen them all," and so forth. This great country with all its bountiful resources cannot afford to join those countries who continue to deny their indigenous peoples their rightful place in the land on which they dwelt long before it was conquered and raped by outsiders—mostly white people.

My Canadian Pacific railroad days were full of hard work and broad experiences, both good and bad, and good rewards. I became such a good porter that I was awarded the "standby" job on weekends during the school term also. This meant that I would get dressed in my uniform and report to the platform of the outgoing train in case an assigned porter was unable to take care of his car. This inevitably meant that he reported drunk for duty.

"Drunk again," Doc Weaver said. "Dat's de last time, am warnin you." Then, turning to me he ordered, "Here boy, take dis car." I then carefully helped the old inebriated colleague to repack his gear and guided him stumbling off the platform.

This was the Saturday night train to Toronto in a Grand car. The Grand series was the top of the luxury line of cars. They were made with beautiful mahogany, brass fittings and comfortable bedrooms, adjoining an elegant bar and dining car. The bed had a set of drawers underneath that held the bed linens. It was there that the porters hid the much-sought Canadian whisky, which was smuggled over to Detroit through Windsor during the US prohibition. It is said that many a Canadian became a millionaire in this trade.

Standing by my Grand car in my starched white jacket and pillbox hat with the step carefully placed at the door, I would put on my best Canadian Pacific Railroad smile and proudly proclaim "First class to Toronto, step this way, watch the step, may I take your bag, sir?" Over and over, saying the well-rehearsed song, knowing that the bonding with these rich passengers had to take place early, as the journey was not really very long. We left at 10 pm and arrived at 6 am. The actual running time was about six hours so a couple of hours were granted as sleep time then breakfast. This night train was mostly for businessmen shuttling between the financial jungles of St James Street to Bay Street. They were really rich guys, the likes of whom I had never met in Canada, and they had plenty of what I wanted most—money! I would make as much in tips on that truncated overnight journey as I would in taking a five-day hotbox full of English grandparents journeying from St John to Vancouver to see their families. So I provided five-star hospitality. I remember watching a handsome, black mustached businessman kiss his wife goodbye tenderly, then I took his bag and showed him his seat. He leaned over, whispered, "Get me a double rye on the rocks and a nice chick," and pressed a $10 bill in my hand. I provided both and thanked God for the precious gift.

The trans-continental summer trips were my lifeline, providing the steady income that I used to pay for my pre-med fees and books. The work was hard, and at night after bedding down my 32 passengers, I would turn off the light and return to the "smoker" to shine my shoes. The smoker was a room with a long bench that served as a smoking area. If anyone wanted their shoes shined they would leave them outside their bunk. I had a special kit, so I quickly developed a shoeshine skill that matched that of any street shine boys.

One night, I had completed my night's tasks in the smoker and on returning my shine kit to the cupboard I spotted a carton of Craven A cigarettes, which a passenger had given to me as a tip. I wondered just how it felt to smoke a cigarette, and I tried one. A large inhalation was followed by a bout of coughing, then a strange floating, rather pleasant feeling. This was the start of my addiction to nicotine which led to my smoking—first cigarettes then a pipe—for the next 50 years. It was a horrible, filthy habit. It caused me to cough incessantly and it discoloured my teeth severely. I made many attempts to stop but succeeded only 10 years ago (see later). Nevertheless

I think that that pipe helped me a great deal in getting through stressful periods of my life. The smoker was also used as a meeting place for porters during the quiet hours of the night. It was there that I got to know many of my fellow porters and discuss many topics with them.

One night a porter from the next car came to my smoker. He was a white lad, a student from a southern black American university with black straight hair and striking good looks, like Tyrone Power. He explained that he was really black; he only looked the way he did by virtue of genetic aberration. He then launched into a vicious diatribe about white people. He told me that I should be careful with whites, never trust them, and never befriend them, especially their women. He explained that their only value to me was in their providing money. He suggested that if any of them hurt me in any way, I should kill them. He demonstrated this with a flick-knife that he had somehow managed to hide from Doc Weaver. He scared me, so I dutifully agreed to heed his advice, gave him a pack of Craven A and bade him goodbye. I found it strange that my most vivid and frightening racial lesson was provided to me by a phenotypically white man.

The porters from McGill were moulded into a special bond, and Johnny M, an Ethiopian, was to become my best friend. The old porters never failed to offer us advice, always about returning to university and never thinking of continuing to porter as a career. They pointed to Professor Melville, a Jamaican doctor who once worked as a porter but was now the professor of pharmacology at McGill. I admit that I was tempted to renounce my doctoring ambitions and continue a career as a porter, but now I'm glad that I didn't.

Those transcontinental trips were in themselves an education equal in value to that which I was receiving at McGill. It seems to me that many of the women travelling alone underwent a drastic change in their behaviour, which manifested itself as a much heightened sexual state. It was as if they considered the porters as convenient, safe, sexual objects. Often at night my bell would ring and I would go to find a nearly completely undressed woman asking some irrelevant question, such as "What time is it?" or "Where are we now, porter?"

In reply I would check my watch, lift up the curtain, stare out into the moonlight and knowingly nod and say "about 60 minutes from Brandon, ma'am". I tried desperately to concentrate on this manoeuvre and not on the lady's exposed breasts, although some of them were rather appealing. Doc Weaver's words rang in my ears:

"Keep your hands off dose white women, boy. Dat's one ting whitey don't like." Mostly, I succeeded.

In the small kitchen I learned how to cook my favorite Jamaican dish—rice and peas. I wasn't quite up to Mattie's standards but my passengers readily bought bowls of it, so adding to my income. To this day I enjoy cooking rice and peas for any unsuspecting guest in my home.

We would arrive in Vancouver in the morning and it was an exciting, joyous time. It was a busy time for me as I had to convert the car again from the sleeping mode to a carriage mode. I was also acutely aware that this was pay-off time—the *raison d'*être of my five days. Despite my inevitable exhaustion and injuries—muscle strains, sore fingertips from smoothing bed linens, and back pain—I had to put my best face forward in a fresh, starched white jacket. As the train clanged to a halt, I would quickly place the box at the foot of the step and loudly announce, "Van-coo-vah, ladies and gentlemen, watch your step and don't forget the porter, working his way through college." "Thank you ma'am, thank you sir, goodbye ma'am, goodbye sir." I developed a special way of helping passengers down by gently taking their arm at the wrist and elbow and holding my left hand across their body in anticipation of the tip. Those who were evidently not going to tip—we called them "stiffs"—would get my not-so-gentle urging. The wrist would be firmly guided around to the back, which provided mild discomfort—but often enough squeezed the tip out of the stiff.

In my fourth and final pre-med year, I still lived in Student House but my participation in house activities diminished markedly. I worked there as the dishwasher, cleaned the toilet and common areas and also removed snow. From my poorly heated room in the attic I would have to hang my head out the window to blow my cigarette smoke out. But the smell persisted. The chief of the fellowship told me that unless I stopped smoking I would have to leave the house. I told him that I would try. Of course I couldn't. So I took long walks at night through the snow and found friendly coffeehouses in which to study. My grades were falling and I was desperately applying to many medical schools—in Canada and the USA, UK, India and Australia. I applied to about 50 medical schools and was refused by all of them. I prepared to go home to Jamaica and to become a beach bum on the north coast. I had one more med school to hear from—McGill. I made repeated trips to the medical faculty office and the dean's secretary, a kind lady called Mrs Mills, got to know my face and I think she could read my anxiety and fear of impending rejection. The admissions board met regularly and the final list was published one afternoon. I ran up to Mrs Mills; she saw me and smiled and winked. I was overjoyed.

I attended my graduation ceremony where I received my Bachelor of Science degree from the vice chancellor. It was a joyful time with proud parents taking photos and many hugs and kisses. I was alone, preparing for my last summer on the Canadian Pacific Railroad. I returned my cap and gown, went into a bar and got very drunk—for the first time. I had not drunk at all up until this time—alcohol was a mortal sin in my home. I staggered along Sherbrooke Street with my degree and its rounded case then I threw it into a melting, dirty snow bank. A few blocks away, I realized what I had done, so I staggered back and retrieved it.

It was lonely in Student House that summer, but I was busy on the Canadian Pacific Railroad journeys. I was now holding down the Montreal to Vancouver run. I had a three-day layover in Vancouver and a six-day rest in Montreal. In this period, I could perform as a standby at Windsor station and pick up overnight trips to places like St John, New Brunswick, Boston, Detroit or Toronto. When I stayed overnight it was in one of the porters' quarters, which were always in the black areas of the town. In St John, New Brunswick, the quarters were called "Niggertown" and I was warned not to stray far from its confines. I was scared shitless so I didn't go out. I was impressed by the density of the black population in this area of St John and the few blacks to whom I was able to speak seemed to be angry, depressed and deprived. It was a sad area, and I was glad to leave. During my Montreal free days, I went to the tennis courts where I would pick up games. Eventually I got a job there as an assistant groundsman. My tennis improved remarkably and indeed I was able to make the odd buck giving lessons to rich kids.

Chapter Seven

MEDICAL SCHOOL

I could hardly wait to start my medical studies. The medical school was a magnificent old building, bursting with history, including Osler's library, where later I worked a night shift. I was anxious to meet my 120 new classmates. We were greeted by the dean, a brilliant, imposing man, Professor G. Lyman Duff, who outlined the academic and behavioural requirements to us.

The first year, in retrospect, was the most difficult of the four years of study. Anatomy, physiology and biochemistry were demanding subjects. The thought of failing any one of these hung like a sword of Damocles over my head and acted as a powerful stimulant to study diligently. I now had a single room in the loft so I was able to study at odd periods at night without disturbing roommates. The most daunting subject in first year was anatomy, taught by an imposing and entertaining Irishman, Dr C.P. Martin. He wore a strange black band around his head with the patch at the back. Word had it that part of his skull had been blown away by an IRA bullet and the patch covered that defect. We never questioned the story and gave him added awe and respect for it. In his first lecture, he explained how we could protect ourselves from catching a cold in three easy steps:

Breathe deeply.

Always end a shower with cold water.

If your nose starts to run, inhale salt water up one nostril and blow it out through the other.

I have followed this advice for the past 58 years and I think it has helped me a lot. Try it!

C.P. described the courses of blood vessels and muscles by pointing out that "they cross over there and carry on down in that particular direction". I had great fun imitating him at various class parties. We were quickly inducted into the temple of horrors—the anatomy lab. It was a cold dungeon-like room where dead bodies lay covered on marble slabs. Five of us worked on one body and we cut various tracks through it until it was completely dismembered. In our first session we were all trying to hide our various emotions: fear, anxiety, nausea and terror under a mantle of bravado, false pride, nonchalance. But what came out were usually nervous giggles and stale jokes.

I had already started to befriend a small group of lads who seemed to be my type—fun-loving, anxious, ambitious. They nominated me for the post of class president.

Each of the nominees gave a presentation of their background and plans for the class if elected. Those running were impressive indeed including football players, fraternity members, musicians, and so forth, and they outlined their aspirations for a class of hard-working serious students on the road to becoming McGill doctors.

I explained that I was a porter for the CPR and if I was elected we would have a party every month with lots of beer and dancing. I was elected and automatically became the vice president of the McGill student society. I enjoyed this post and our parties were renowned as the best at McGill at that time. I also had a short period working for the student newspaper, *The McGill Daily*. I wrote headlines for articles and on slack days our editor, John Scott, told me "We need some letters to the editor, Colin. Write about rowdy McGill students." I started a steady stream of letters to the editor about drunken students hollering down McTavish and Peel streets on weekends. I would sign them "Disgusted" or "Mother of Four".

By midterm about six of us had formed a group that was to bond even closer all through medical school years. Members were Monty Fox, Mark Peterson, Dave Brown, Suki Iwojama, Johnny Martin, Jerry Schonfeld and me. Cal Gormky, Don Tolbert, Charlie Shaver and Jack Phanon often joined us.

Med. School classmates.

Jerry was a fun-loving lad of superior intellect and a fine musician. He was also severely lacking in moral judgement and given to excessive alcohol consumption. He came from a wealthy American family and had an upscale apartment house near the medical school on Prince Arthur Street and Lorne Avenue. He asked me to come to share his apartment with him—at no cost if I could get him through the first year of medical school. I quickly accepted that offer because my lifestyle had changed to the degree that it was no longer compatible with my residence at Student House. I had begun to drink Molson's Pilsner and my cigarette consumption had increased.

Our gang life was centred around Jerry's apartment. We had several parties there with a now fully fledged orchestra consisting of Jerry on the piano or trumpet, Dave Brown on the trombone, Johnny Martin or me on the drums. At the time there was no shortage of girls for our parties, mostly working girls from the neighbourhood. Once Jerry decided to invite some student nurses from the Royal Victoria Hospital. We agreed, with much reservation, as these girls had the reputation of being high class and standoffish and we wondered how they would fit in with our raucous behaviour. Jerry as usual bought all the beer and bottles of Teacher's Highland Cream and sloe gin. He also decided to serve some canapés that he made with cat food and Worcestershire sauce. The girls seemed to enjoy it! We had only one large double bed, which I shared with Jerry. So many a night I had to sleep on the couch while one or other of Jerry's consorts took my half of the bed.

We had regular exams all through the term, which would jolt us out of our merriment and curtail our parties. So we would gather around the dining table and do serious 24-hour studying. The format was to go through the class notes (from those who attended) and the relevant section of the textbook. We would take turns to sleep and after one or two hours the sleeper would return to the table, then the next in line would summarize all that had gone on while he had been in bed. That worked remarkably well and we all got through our final exams in the first year. In fact, although Jerry attended few classes of a course in public health called Health and Social Medicine, he came first in that exam.

Our anatomy final consisted of a written text and the all-important practical test (spots). In the test, specimens of bones, muscles, organs or vessels would be laid out on a table and we would move to each specimen every time the bell was rung. It was reputed to be the most difficult exam of the entire medical course and one had to pass it to continue. We were all scared of this exam, so Jerry came up with his version of the ideal solution. He devised a unique way of emulating the spots. We drilled ourselves and all of us passed.

Histology was taught by a man from France named Professor Guy LeBlond. He had a Maurice Chevalier accent and a pronounced French sense of humour. When teaching us about the penis, he drew a long line across all three sections of the blackboard, curved the end and followed it back to the start. Then he stepped back, looked at this tubular object that he had drawn, rubbed his hands together and soulfully said "I seenk zat I ave been a beet too generous". We cheered! He imbued the cells of every organ with fascinating properties that enabled us to understand the important aspects of the function of that organ: the adrenal gland, the liver, the thyroid, the skin.

I feared biochemistry because chemistry had not been one of my favourite subjects in secondary school. Our teacher, Professor A.B. Thompson, was a highly intellectual Englishman with a wry sense of humour and a twinkle in his eye. He made sense of complex reactions like the Krebs or tricarboxylic acid cycle, the structure of the steroid ring, the complex metabolism of sugars and amino-acid chains. He was able to instil in me the desire and ability to understand all these complicated chemical processes and to demonstrate in my exam that I had done so. I got an A in biochemistry and that made me feel proud.

I was having a difficult time adjusting to the academic rigours of that first year. I sought advice from an English chap who was graduating just as I was entering first year. "Any tips on getting through first year?" I asked.

"Play squash every day, me lad," he shouted. I was not a good squash player but I found much enjoyment and exercise in playing tennis by myself against the wall of a doubles squash court. I kept healthy in this way even though it meant I would have to trudge through the snow to the Sir Arthur Curry gym at night. I am sure that this helped me a lot to get through my first year.

As a reward, my father gave me a trip back to Jamaica. I was overjoyed at the prospect so I celebrated the night before by partying all night. My plan was to leave early in the morning. But after hurried last-minute packing I fell asleep and awoke far too close to my departure time with a horrible hangover. I called the airport and explained that I was a prominent neurosurgeon with an emergency call to Jamaica and requested that the plane wait for me. No promise was given but after a hair-raising taxi drive I arrived at Dorval Airport in the nick of time. I slept most of the journey and awoke for a meal that was served just before landing. It looked attractive so I gobbled it down, only to become violently sick afterwards. The meal was lobster and shrimp and this was my introduction to a severe crustacean allergy that was to follow me the rest of my life. Strangely, my favourite food in childhood in Jamaica had been shrimp and rice, which Matty had prepared superbly. The lesson I learned is that anyone can become allergic to anything at any time. On landing in Jamaica I was greeted by a large group of family and friends with much jubilation but I was a sad sight—hung over, just recovering from a severe food reaction and generally wiped out. I got home and slept for a long time.

I awoke to a magnificent Jamaican food meal prepared by Matty. As in many other cultures, our food traditions in Jamaica are deeply rooted. One of the staple dishes is salt fish and ackee. Ackee is a strange vegetable whose brilliant yellow, red and black colours belie its bland taste, which resembles avocado. It is used to offset the sharp stringent taste of salted cod fish. For centuries the fish was imported in dried slab-like form from Newfoundland and Nova Scotia in exchange for spices, bananas, sugar and rum from Jamaica. Salt fish was cheap so it was a poor man's food; today it is expensive and out of reach of the poor. The other staple food was rice and peas, a delightful dish of rice cooked in a big pot with coconut milk and various spices. This method invariably left a layer of slightly burned rice stuck to the bottom of the pot, called "bun rice". It was my favourite, so Matty always had a dish of it put aside for me.

Many years later I was at a sumptuous buffet laid out in grand style at one of Kingston's upmarket international hotels and I noticed a bowl of bun rice among the fine foods on display—others must like it too! We had a great family dinner with the family now extended to include Peter, my sister's fiancé.

I could not help noticing that my parents had become intensely religious and our home was the headquarters for a number of itinerant foreign missionaries. "The Forbes Hotel" one of them joked. I welcomed most of them as they were good fun to be with. Some were obviously racist and I shunned those. My father and I occasionally had heated arguments on my new-found views about Jamaican society—its colour code, its exploitation of poor blacks, its lingering colonialism. My mother was opposed to us speaking the Jamaican patois in the home. My parents thought I was becoming a communist. In fact, at McGill I had been befriended by members of the Communist party, masquerading under innocuous names such as the Cosmo Club. My main attraction to the communists was one or two buxom lasses who seemed to enjoy my company—they laughed at my jokes! One even invited me to her house for dinner but the invitation had to be cancelled at the last minute because her parents had decided to return home early from Florida—an opportunity for couch wrestling missed.

Another problem I had in Jamaica was my cigarette smoking. Smoking was strictly forbidden in our house and I was now a confirmed addict. I had to sneak outside for my puffs and of course I was caught. I explained that these were special cigarettes prescribed by a doctor in Montreal for my asthma.

During this holiday Jamaica was hit by a strong hurricane. We got a couple days warning so we boarded up our windows and made other preparations. During the hurricane my father called me over to a window to see small huts, doors, roofs and trees floating by our house. The next morning the wind settled and my dad and I drove around the town, amazed at the terrible destruction. We tried to get to the airport road, the Palisades, and we saw a large ship blocking the road. Our fear was for my sisters, who were attending a Christian girls' camp at Moorlands in the middle of the island. We decided to drive to fetch them. It was a harrowing drive but we eventually reached them and they were all safe, so we brought them home. As we drove, I realized that a hurricane, like many other natural disasters, is scary and inconvenient for the rich but truly destructive and even fatal for the poor. A few nights after the hurricane, when I had finished my hard day's work of clearing up our own compound, I decided to take a trip in our car to the nearest bar. I had never drunk alcohol in Jamaica so this was a new experience.

After a few hurried rum drinks I was on my way home when I saw a woman at the bus stop. I offered her a ride, which she gladly accepted. We chatted about the hurricane and I offered to show her the ship on the road to Port Royal. Again, she gladly accepted and explained that she was a nurse and her husband was a medical student in America. I got more and more sexually aroused as we spoke and apparently she did also. By the time we reached the ship we could hardly contain ourselves and we had violent sexual intercourse in the front seat in the car parked in the shadow of the beached ship, under the moon. This was my first sexual experience and I was amazed at the intensity of its emotions. Little wonder, I thought, that it made people, men especially, behave in strange ways rarely accepted by society. I thought of the king of England, Edward the VIII, giving up his throne just so he could have regular sexual intercourse with a beautiful American divorcee. That first experience was to affect me for the rest of my life as I came to regard sexual intercourse as the most beautiful emotion in one's life and potentially one of the most dangerous and destructive.

I was anxious to return to medical school so we had the requisite ritual going-away ceremonies, mostly deeply religious but some quite fun and enjoyable. Somehow I found that a number of the young ladies of the group were quite attracted to me. I did not regard myself as a "catch", mostly because of my dark skin colour, but it was a boost to my ego to realize that some beautiful Jamaican girls found me attractive. I never even considered them as potential sexual partners because at that time in my opinion (and that of many others), this world was divided into two types of women: those to screw and those to marry.

I returned to Montreal and continued my raucous life at Jerry's apartment. Inevitably my academic performance suffered and my marks went down and down. I certainly threw myself into the "fun" part of student life. Our core group had now devised a unique pattern—fool around for most of the time, then a month before exams study intensely at Jerry's apartment. Our fooling around consisted mostly of nights on end drinking at the Shrine, a beer house just near the university that was mostly inhabited by students. We were the main medical representatives. We drank beer—mine was Molson's pilsner by the quart bottle. We sometimes pretended to study but mostly we took our drinking seriously and interspersed it with tales of experiences (mostly lies), dirty jokes and wild plans for our future.

Johnny Martin occasionally ranted about Africa, its sad colonial history, its exciting independent present, its great leaders (Haile Selassie, Kwame Nkruma, Jomo Kenyatta, Dr Hastings Banda, Julius Nyerere). I listened intently to his version of African affairs, which was often completely different from that of the media. For example, Jomo Kenyatta was described as a depraved murderer of kind white people but Johnny Martin told me that he was the liberator of millions of human beings from vicious colonial oppression.

Johnny was pivotal in my life. He reformed my ideas on race and colonialism and slowly I began to take pride in my African ancestry. I threw myself whole-heartedly into the emerging struggle for independence that was sweeping over Africa and the Caribbean. I became a follower of Ghandi's non-violent movement and Martin Luther King was my newfound hero. His "Dream" speech was to replace the Sermon on the Mount and "Ode to Daffodils" (Wordsworth) as my all-time favourites of English language expression. I bought a framed copy of this Dream speech and it has always hung in the entrance hall of the homes I have had all over the world.

Winter came and we continued our wild life of second-year medicine. The class parties continued, as I had promised in my election speech. I performed at each of them, mostly doing caricatures of our teachers or telling shaggy-dog stories with the occasional dirty joke thrown in. Here is a song I composed for one of our second-year parties. Tune, "Glow Little Glow Worm":

I'm just a second-year medical student
Our behaviour is not very prudent...
and so forth.

At my 50th class reunion, instead of following the proscribed pattern of describing how great we and our families were I sang this song. It did not receive unanimous applause.

We seemed to have excuses not to study. At one stage we began skipping classes and we went from one bar to another, playing pinball machines. Mark Peterson was the expert. Jerry always tilted and I just couldn't get the flashing lights. Our shenanigans got worse and worse. One weekend Jesse decided that we should play a new game, "Hold the Phone". The game consisted of dialing a random number at a public phone booth and when it answered we would shout, "Hold the phone", yank it off its cage and run away wildly. After awhile, we collected quite a few telephone receiver sets in our apartment, which we regarded as kind of a *prix d'guerre*. In retrospect, this was a tribute to our uninhibited state that several quarts of Molson's placed on us.

Perhaps the most enjoyable and least destructive activity in which we engaged was the jazz band. We played at the student union for the Cosmo Club or the African and Caribbean Club dances. Once in the early spring, Jerry decided that he would put down the roof of his Oldsmobile 88 convertible and drive around town blaring our music. It was well received by a rather confused Montreal public. At a carnival dance in the middle of winter, Johnny decided that we should dance down Sherbrook Street behind the Oldsmobile wearing the colobus monkey skins that usually covered his living room floor. That was well received. Johnny usually spent the night playing drums with the band. That left his wife, Rose, all alone.

Jazz Band.

Rose was the daughter of a Jamaican single mother born in Montreal. She was brought up in the strict rural Jamaican tradition on St Antoine Street. She was close to the family of Oscar Peterson and she once set up a date for me with Oscar's sister. That didn't work out. Rose was a stunningly beautiful woman with an engaging smile and the cutest dimples you ever did see! It was a pleasure for me to dance with her while her husband pounded away on the drums, Teacher's Highland Cream whiskey close at hand. In fact Ruth taught me how to dance the exotic, rhythmic, movement of the calypso, reggae and some Latin dances.

It is prudent for me to follow Johnny's life at this time. He eventually graduated with us and interned with the group of us at St Mary's hospital in Montreal. I shall dwell on this period later. He even spent a short time in Washington DC with his sister, who was married to the Ethiopian ambassador to the USA. His family was close to that of Emperor Haile Selassie and Johnny's father was a doctor who became His Majesty's ambassador to England while they were all living there during the Italian occupation of Ethiopia. Dr Martin Senior as a child was found abandoned in a battlefield by a Scottish doctor called Dr Martin, taken to Scotland and brought up in that family who put him through medical school. Johnny was the first Ethiopian to become a doctor. He returned to Ethiopia and had five children, Johnny being the youngest. The family lived in Addis Ababa but also had a home in Nazareth, an ancient town outside of Addis. Johnny attended school in England and the American University of Beirut then came to McGill.

During the Italian occupation, Johnny's father was to witness the execution of most of his family by the Italians in retribution for the assassination of a prominent Italian officer. Many educated Ethiopians were executed at that time. So Johnny's father and his family fled to the UK along with Haile Selassie and his family where they remained until the Italians eventually were driven out of Ethiopia. Notably, Haile Selassie addressed the League of Nations (a precursor to the UN) and warned them of the impending fascist movement and the necessity to stop its spread. Unfortunately the warning was not heeded and the Second World War ensued. At that time Europe was evidently unwilling to heed the prophetic warnings delivered to them from a small brown man.

Johnny's father and Haile Selassie returned to Ethiopia after the war and His Majesty tried desperately to rebuild his broken country and bring it from the tatters of colonial occupation to a modern state of the 20th century. He was also the primary force in the founding of the Organization of African Unity (OAU) with its headquarters in Addis Ababa.

Johnny returned to Ethiopia after Washington. He embarked on post-graduate studies in obstetrics and gynecology. He did some training in Sweden, a country that had a close relationship with Ethiopia, providing much assistance in medical training and services. Johnny became adept at the repair of vesico-vaginal fistula, a scourge of Ethiopian women, many of whom spent days in obstructed labour with the presenting part of the foetus banging on the pelvic wall and creating connection between the bladder and rectum. If the woman survived, she was destined to spend her life incontinent of urine and faeces, thus ensuring her social status as a social outcast. Johnny's radical method of V-V repair provided a new life for many Ethiopian women.

At this time His Majesty appointed Johnny as his personal physician as had been his father. This meant that Johnny accompanied His Majesty on his many overseas trips. Johnny also served with the UN forces in Congo during the rebellion of Lumumba. He was in Leopoldville when a force of angry rebels threatened to kill a group of foreigners, mostly American missionaries who had taken refuge in a church. Johnny faced the angry mob and explained that these foreigners had nothing to do with them and if they were going to kill anyone, it should be he, an African, and not the white foreigners. The rebels left in disgust and the white people escaped.

He was awarded the Congressional Medal of Honor for that.

Ironically, Ethiopia was to suffer under a new leader, General Hailu Mengistu. He purported to save the country from the oppressive rule of His Majesty Haile Selassie. He embarked on a slow revolution and gradually stripped the emperor of his power, then imprisoned him. It is said that he kept His Majesty in a cage directly beneath the desk at which he sat. Johnny was ordered to continue to provide care for the imprisoned emperor. Once when His Majesty was gravely ill Johnny raved at his captors and shouted that they should just kill him rather than prolong his suffering and indignity. The officer ordered that Johnny be shot so he was taken out and the firing squad was marched out. He refused to be blindfolded and shouted for them to shoot him quickly. The officer in charge of the squad approached Johnny and said "Dr Johannes, you cared for my wife, you must go away quickly". So he escaped certain death. Johnny was the bravest man I have ever known. I respected him and loved him dearly.

We were not close during those times—but he did visit me once in Kenya and we went down to our lovely cottage on Diani Beach. It rained incessantly, so we spent three days with some Teacher's Highland Cream exchanging our experiences. This is when I learned the stories that I have just written. He returned to me in 2002, suffering from prostate hypertrophy, which was operated on. A blood test also revealed an early form of myeloid leukemia, which caused his demise a year later. I went to Addis for his burial. The Amharic orthodox funeral rites were long and severe. I cried incessantly during the continuous wailing. I was asked to assist in carrying the casket down a long flight of stone steps to the family vault below the cathedral. I was completely emotionally overcome and I hardly made it back up the stairs. Johnny's three girls were behind me and gave me much comfort and love. One of their sons had mercy on me and sneaked me to a big hotel to feed me some Jamaican rum. As you can see, Johnny M had a profound influence on my life and the lessons he taught me about race, pride and nationalism versus jingoism, loyalty versus "hanging on for the ride", and many other things have helped tremendously to shape my own beliefs and actions.

Needless to say our second year was as disastrous academically as it was exciting and fun socially. We realized, rather too late, that the exams were imminent so we drew up a study plan. As before, we took turns at sleeping with adequate revision on returning to the table. Alcohol consumption was minimized and only beer was allowed. This led to the usual disastrous effect on the gaseous bowel admissions, causing us to attempt a strategy that would allow us to continue studying and not collapse in respiratory and olfactory disgust with each loud emission. Monty Fox taught us to lean back in our chairs with our legs drawn up on our chest and fire the gas out at the same time holding a lighted match as close as safely possible to our clothed anal orifice. When he first demonstrated this technique, a huge blue flame shot out from his bottom to the amazement of us all. We laughed and shouted and screamed in delight at this fantastic accomplishment. A couple of years later, when we were due to graduate, we all went for the time-honoured ritual of the yearbook picture and then presented our short biography along with the personal motto. Every one of our gang listed among our activities "member of the Blue Flame Club". This was in stark contrast to the rest of the class, whose listings included "member of the McGill Yacht Club" or "Fencing Club" or "Choral Society" or a Greek-lettered fraternity. My children express incongruous amusement when I describe what the Blue Flame Club was, but I do not demonstrate!

In the second year my marks dropped considerably. I was called up to Dr C.P.'s office. He asked me why my academic performance had dropped. I told him that I was unsure but I promised to correct that in the next year. He said that whatever it was, he was sure that I needed funds and quietly slipped $200 into my hands—an enormous amount of money for me at that time. He attached two provisos to this gift: 1) I should tell no one about it, 2) I must do the same for two other people sometime in my life. Fortunately, I have been able to do this for many more than a hundred people up to now. You may recognize this as the basis of several micro-finance movements, most of which have been enormously successful. The author Lloyd C. Douglas, who wrote the *Magnificent Obsession,* was once the minister of a church in Montreal and it is said that he based that story on C.P. Martin's works.

I continued to work at the CPR in my holidays but it became evident that I would have to spend more time studying so my railway hours during term time had to be curtailed. I learned about a program being presented by the Canadian military to students at McGill. It was the Regular Officers Training Program (ROTP) in which the student would enrol in the army as a training officer for three years, then upon graduation would serve as a regular officer for three years. I learned that it was open to Commonwealth students also. I was still a citizen of Jamaica with a British passport. I eagerly pursued this exciting prospect, which would surely solve the formidable financial problems I faced. All three branches of the military, the Navy, Army and Air Force, were recruiting for this program. I started with the Navy. The recruiting officer took one look at me and informed me that I was "not suitable". I later learned that this decision was based on my colour. Non-whites were not welcome in the program. I applied to the Air Force and made a stupid mistake of ticking the "yes" box under "asthma". In fact, I did have recurrent wheezing attacks in my first year. They were usually on Thursday nights after my prolonged exposure to the poor cat that we were experimenting on during physiology lab. To this day I have respiratory and emotional difficulties around cats—I hate them. Naturally, I was rejected by the Air Force on medical grounds.

The Army was my only hope left, and I hoped and prayed for acceptance. One afternoon I had a telephone call ordering me to report to the Quebec Army Headquarters on Atwater Street to see the prominent French Canadian head of the unit. Shaky and sweaty, I was led into the presence of an imposing mustached general of French Canadian persuasion. He had just returned from lunch (three martinis?) and was in high spirits. He seemed genuinely glad to see me and was talkative. "Now, Forbes," he said, "I want you to know that the Army is a difficult place in which to work and live. It was hard for me as a Frenchman to reach the position that I now hold. I have been called all the names—Frenchie, Pea Soup, and so forth, but I did not let that worry me. I was determined to become the best officer in the Canadian Army, and I made it! Now, if you're in the officers mess with a bunch of drunk officers, and one of them calls you 'nigger' what are you going to do?"

"I shall look at him, do and say nothing, then walk away," I said.

"That's right, Forbes. Congratulations and do your best."

Officer training at Camp Borden.

Camp Borden bedroom.

I had been accepted and virtually blessed by the highest officer in the command. Seven years later, when I was the regiment's medical officer for the Royal Canadian Dragoons in Iserlohn, West Germany, I was ordered to Soest to see the general. "Yes, Forbes," he said. "I have been following your career. You have done well, I'm proud of you."

"That's all because of you, sir. I am deeply thankful," I said, with a snappy old-time open-hand salute.

Of course, I was overjoyed at my acceptance, but it was not well received by my buddies. They accused me of joining the "killing squad" and they predicted that I would be thrown out for fooling around too much, or running away in battle.

All this changed when I received my first paycheck—a whopping $800, representing months of back pay, book and uniform allowance, and a monthly living allowance. I foolishly announced this to the gang and it was received with loud and raucous acclaim. A hastily held meeting made the decision to celebrate this windfall that same night with a party at Rockhead's Paradise Café. The now-expanded group met at this sacred watering hole on St Antoine Street, the black ghetto of Montreal. The owner, Rufus Rockhead (an ex porter), was most pleased to welcome us when he heard the news of my windfall. His anticipation of a good sale that night was quickly realized. The kick line of scantily dressed black women, Sweets and the Rockadettes performed superbly for us that night. I paid the huge bill, staggered home and kept counting the small change in my pocket and wondering where all the rest of the money had gone! That night I was rudely awakened by Jerry, who ordered me out of my side of the bed as he gently bedded Sweets in my place. I staggered to the couch and remained there for the next 12 hours.

Exams were strenuous. About three weeks before them, we set the schedule of study, which we vowed to follow—realizing that our very future depended on our success. We banned poker games, the Rockheads, the Swiss Hut—our favourite new watering hole—pinball machines and we drastically reduced our sessions at the Shrine. One essential activity persisted—a regular visit to Francine's whorehouse. We would call and book an appointment for all of us en bloc. We would take our class notes and march into Francine's apartment and settle ourselves in the waiting room. One by one we were called in to perform our essential and vital duty. Francine came to know me as the poor black boy who needed mothering more than fucking and she provided that between her ample breasts.

I never had a "steady" girlfriend in this period. At our drunken parties I would sometimes pick up enough courage to ask a girl to dance. Usually after a few cute Caribbean moves, I would step on her toes and retreat to flop into a chair against the wall. Alcohol was certainly the stuff on which I leaned heavily and the club that clobbered me over my head. It certainly contributed to my resounding failures in relationships with women. It caused me to have a strong feeling of unworthiness and a king-sized inferiority complex. Whenever I looked at women who appeared attractive to me, I would tell myself, "Forget it, man, she would never look at a drunken, black bum like you."

At the same time, I felt a certain sense of freedom, which I valued, especially when I witnessed the problems my friend Johnny, who was married, or the others who had steady girlfriends were constantly facing—mostly due to infidelity or drunkenness.

Chapter Eight

THE ARMY

My summers were spent in officer training at the Royal Canadian Army Medical Corps school—Camp Borden. This was again a time of hard work, physical and mental, good friendships and heavy drinking. All the officer cadets were medical students from all over Canada. Again, I was the only black. Never did I experience racial discrimination in any form—we were all there to learn how to become good officers in Her Majesty's RCAMC. We slept on spartan beds in a simple room where there was a place for everything. The bed had to be prepared in a specific way—with folds and tucks according to Her Majesty's measurement. Some of the officer cadets slept on the unmade bed or on the floor to gain extra sleeping time in the morning instead of labouring to make up the bed to Queen's regulation orders. Our boots had to be highly polished, and we wrapped the ends of our trousers over our boots with a thick band called a puttee. The day began with a spartan breakfast followed by a morning parade, which included a rigid inspection of our rooms and a presentation on the parade square. Our trainer was Sgt Latullippe. We would be sharply rebuffed if we called him "sir". "I'm not sir," he would shout, "I am sergeant. You bums will be sirs, God help us." He would inspect us as we stood as stiffly as we could to attention. One of his favourite observations was, "Sir, you're bleeding from your eyeballs," to the hung-over cadets. He would stand behind an officer cadet and say "Sir, am I hurting you?"

"No, Sergeant."

"Well I should be because I'm stepping on your hair—get a haircut!"

A particularly diabolic activity was the "route march". We would be in full "battle dress" with a heavy pack on our backs containing all one needs to survive for several weeks, and a heavy Lee-Enfield rifle. We marched for many miles with few rest periods. Fortunately, the French-speaking members of our company had an endless supply of songs, which we quickly learned and marched by. After awhile I learned that these words were the most vile curse words in the French language, many of which alluded to sacred church functions such as the chalice and the tabernacle. These songs became the favourites at the nightly sessions at the bar. Occasionally when I tired of the French songs I would render my drunken version of "Day-O", invariably accompanied by my long-drawn-out explanation of my association with Harry Belafonte in my class at Wolmer's in Jamaica. That certainly impressed the gang at the bar, and pulled me up a couple of notches in the scale of regimental importance.

Fortunately, I was able to pass all the exams necessary to graduate from officer training school. I bluffed my way through the tactical army manoeuvre exam. Luckily, I excelled in the public speaking exam. We had to speak on a topic of our choice. My presentation was "How to Grow a Mustache". I outlined, with illustrations on the blackboard, the different shapes and types of mustaches. Then I explained the various methods necessary to grow one successfully. At this time, my mustache was thick and black and well trimmed—very military. I explained that it resulted from scrupulous daily application of a magic oil. This caught the undivided attention of the class and afterwards, more than one fellow cadet surreptitiously asked me for the name of this "magic oil". This oil was all a product of my imagination, but I had to come up with an answer, so I told them it was Vicks Vaporub.

The big day came when we had our graduation ceremony—the "marching out parade". I had been appointed the company sergeant major for the parade—a prominent and responsible position. I proudly led my company to the strains of a rousing military band. We all received our commissions in the Army. That night, we had a big ball in the gym. We imported girls from Toronto for the occasion and they arrived by bus, all shining and beautiful. For the first time we were allowed to wear an officer's uniform, a smart khaki-coloured serge suit with an over-the-shoulder Sam Browne belt. This event was the pinnacle of my Army career to date and I certainly celebrated that night—getting even more drunk than usual. I somehow found a lass who would dance more than once with me, so I accompanied her on the bus to Toronto, which left at about 4 am. It was a long ride and after awhile I gave up wrestling with my date and fell into an alcoholic stupor. I was awakened in the empty bus at the station in Toronto, and I spent quite awhile in the washroom trying to wake up and get properly dressed.

We had received our pay, so I wandered around Toronto until I found a coffeehouse. My address book had a contact phone number for my mother's younger sister, Aunt Ivy, in Hamilton, so I called and was warmly invited to her place. Fortuitously, it was the wedding day of my cousin Harry. He was a blonde white son of my Aunt Emma, whose husband was a rich white American who had died during an appendectomy operation. Harry was a constant rival to me and always subtly lauded his colour "superiority" over me. He was getting married to a white Jamaican lass. I arrived by bus in Hamilton and went directly to the church to catch the tail end of the ceremony.

Afterwards, Aunt Ivy invited me to join in the family photo. Self-consciously, I tried to bury myself in the back of the crowd, as I did not want to compromise the photo with my obvious dark skin—the only one so endowed. The photographer was an energetic, loud, pretty, buxom mid-thirties woman. Surprisingly I heard her shout "Soldier, stand forward a bit and look happy!" I obeyed. After the photos, the photographer came to me and asked me to get her a drink. I brought a half-empty champagne bottle and two glasses. We clinked and connected. Soon she was dragging me downstairs into the basement of the armoury, which was lined with large, upright lockers. We did some heavy necking and when we heard an approaching noise she dragged me into the locker. In short order I was feeding on her breasts and then we started to make love— standing up. The way the lockers were constructed, their stability was certainly no match to our rhythmic, then ecstatic convulsions, so the noise became quite considerable. Finally, exhausted, we were ejected from the locker when its door opened suddenly. We quickly put ourselves together then returned to the wedding party upstairs. She was my first sexual encounter in North America and it certainly taught me some lessons: 1) Canadian women could be very aggressive, even acrobatic lovers, 2) I could not be all that repulsive to women if she could pick me out for this wild adventure. Upstairs, I joined my relatives for the first time. Aunt Ivy was kind to me and seemed to be genuinely happy to see me. She said that I looked handsome in my army uniform. We had several dances together. Her children were all friendly to me and I was glad to have had the opportunity to meet these relatives in their homeland. I returned to Camp Borden, packed and went back to Montreal.

FOURTH YEAR AND INTERNSHIP

My final year in McGill medical was just as wild as the previous three. The clinical studies were now most important and we tried desperately to develop our clinical skills. We attended and sometimes were allowed to scrub for operations and deliveries. I attended the famous Montreal Neurological Institute and watched Dr Wilder Penfield do his groundbreaking brain surgery. I weighed sponges for Dr Vineberg as he performed his internal mammary artery transplants at the Royal Vic. The Montreal General Hospital was then in a rather seedy part of town and we went there for our lessons in dermatology and venereology. I was most surprised when we first visited the venereal disease clinics. A number of women were lying down in the lithotomy position, that is, legs up and spread apart. A sheet covered their faces and separated us. Our teacher would stand at the bottom of the bed to examine a patient's private parts with gloved hands, pointing out the various sores that characterized their disease, such as syphilis, gonorrhoea, chlamydia, herpes. He was strangely friendly (optimistic and kind) and addressed almost all of the patients by name: "Hi Gigi, you're looking better today" or "Fifi, take it easy until these wounds are all healed and don't forget your medications!"

Their responses were as friendly and upbeat: "OK Doc!" or "See you next week," or "Take care, Doc!". I was impressed by the way in which this brilliant man could be so kind, gentle and considerate to these outcasts of society suffering from such horrible diseases. That lesson has remained with me.

Our experience in obstetrics was quite the opposite. I was taught by a doctor at the Royal Victoria Hospital, the upper-class hospital on the hill. Our teacher was a tall, big, overbearing man with a deep voice and a cynical sneer. One morning he was teaching our small group, about five fourth-year students, how to examine a woman in labour. He showed us how to palpate the abdomen, to judge the height of the uterus if possible, to feel the contractions. He then proceeded to show us how to judge the dilation of the cervix through a rectal exam. He explained in a booming voice that the patient was a 17-year-old unmarried girl who was a "primip". He inserted his enormous index finger into her rectum and scooped it all around to define the edge of the cervix to estimate its circumference as 10 centimetres, which was full dilatation. He then ordered all of us to do the same. The girl's face was covered but I saw jerky movements of her abdomen then realized that she was sobbing uncontrollably. I pointed this out to the doctor. He sneered and growled, "Let's move on this". Then he gave us a short talk about "silly girls who get knocked up and can't stand the consequences".

I was extremely upset about this doctor's behaviour which I judged to be inhumane, cruel and unworthy of McGill. I expressed these concerns to members of my class and a few of them joined in with a report of the behaviour to the dean of the medical school. We heard nothing about the outcome but none of us did very well in obstetrics, and few of the class chose obstetrics as a specialty.

The spring of 1955 burst out in true Montreal splendor, but it also brought the terrifying reality of final exams. Our group of seven held a summit meeting at the Shrine. We listened to Pierre the waiter's exotic tales of a winter holiday in Florida and guzzled down several quart bottles of Molson's. We agreed on our strategy for the final exam study schedule—study, sleep, review, then food at the

Greasy Spoon or the Swiss Hut. No more fooling around or visits to the brothel.

We were preparing well into the last desperate push when the catastrophe occurred. One weekend Jerry suddenly left Montreal, McGill and his almost four years of medical studies. We were flabbergasted—the brilliant, surely genius, young man with albeit a strange behaviour pattern would opt to leave the profession he had chosen at a time when he had almost achieved his goal. I was left alone in his apartment. A number of young ladies and seedy men came by to inquire as to his whereabouts. I could honestly say "I don't know".

The most touching was a visit by Charlie the Chinese man who did our laundry. He unloaded an enormous cloth bag from his shoulder, unpacked my laundry and Jerry's, which was considerably bigger than mine. I paid him for mine and I explained that Jerry had gone. He tearfully told me that Jerry owed him for past unpaid laundry bills—a considerable amount, about $80, I think. I explained that I could not pay that but I would see if we all could help to settle the bill. The group of us did just that over the next few weeks. It brought us great joy to see the smile return to Charlie's face.

None of us heard from Jerry until about 50 years later, when Dave Brown met him in California with the Japanese lady who looked after him. He had worked as a laboratory technician.

The final exams eventually came and we dutifully attended and tried to do our best. At the end I was tired, scared and terrified at the thought that I might have failed. On the appointed day I rushed up to the medical building to read the results as posted on the notice board. I elbowed my way to the board and rapidly scanned down to the Fs—and there it was! My name for all to see that I was now a doctor!

I ran across the road to the nearest bar (the Pines) and gulped down a quart of Molson then stumbled back to my room at Mrs Clarke's boarding house, where I had moved after the lease at Jerry's apartment had expired. I flopped on the bed and went off to sleep, only to be awakened by Mrs Clarke for a telephone call. I stumbled downstairs and was greeted by a voice that said "Hello Dr Forbes. Congratulations, I just read your name in the *Montreal Gazette* McGill graduate page. I'm Andrew from *London Life* and I would like to meet you to discuss life insurance."

"Thank you so much, Mr Wood, you're the first person to recognize me as a real doctor and I shall most certainly buy one of your policies." I did just that and I still have this policy of $6000 today plus considerable dividends.

I phoned around and found the few members of the group of seven who were still in Montreal—Johnny Martin, Monty Fox, Dave Brown—and we decided that the best way to celebrate was to go to Montreal's famous amusement centre, Belmont Park, for a huge night on the town! We met and primed ourselves with several beers then decided that the most appropriate activity would be to take a ride in the roller coaster. I had never done this before but I was in no condition to refuse. I vaguely remember pummelling down in the seat while my stomach contents flew up past my face! We then went back to Mrs Clarke's where she sat us down to a meal of *tortiere* and beer. She sat beside me and squeezed my thighs while she told me just how much she loved me from the day she first saw me and how she wished I could crawl into her bed that night as her husband would surely be out drunk on the couch.

Traditionally McGill grads fought hard to get an internship at either the Montreal General Hospital or the Royal Victoria Hospital, McGill's revered and prestigious teaching hospitals. In 1955, however, a substantial number of our graduate class decided to shun these institutions and intern elsewhere. This was no doubt in response to the widespread complaints about the human rights abuses exhibited by some of the teachers at these hospitals. About 10 of us decided to intern at St Mary's Hospital, a small Catholic hospital in the suburbs of Montreal.

The year before, in my final year, I got a job as the night laboratory technician there. My duties consisted of doing all the emergency lab work ordered after hours. Work included difficult tasks such as determining blood urea levels by the long, drawn-out method and serial hourly blood sugars on patients with diabetic ketoacidosis. Test kits and machines, now in routine use, were not available in those days, so I commonly lost a whole night's sleep carrying out these monotonous tasks.

Another one of my duties was to assist in post-mortem exams. I had to wheel the body along on a stretcher to the post-mortem room, open up the abdomen, wash out the gut and remove the top of the skull. The pathologist, anxious to get the bodies prepared quickly, would complain loudly if I was going too slowly. I also had to put up with the remonstrations of the funeral parlor morticians who collected the bodies. They always dressed in black suits and smelled of liquor. "How are the femorals?" they would shout at me. "Hope you didn't fuck them up again." They injected their magic embalming potions through these vessels.

One night a particularly fun-loving ward nurse suggested that they take me down to the post-mortem room on a stretcher duly shrouded. I complied with the gruesome request and was wheeled down on the stretcher by the nurse and my fellow intern Johnny Martin. On arrival, I was surrounded by the awaiting students and staff, and I quickly sat up on the trolley and came to life! The expected consternation was of great amusement to us. The matron nun on night duty hid her enjoyment as she reprimanded us in typical Irish fashion.

One of my fellow interns was a short, slightly built Japanese Canadian named Suki Iwamura. He sometimes drank with us and after half a bottle of beer would repeatedly describe the horrible indignities and punishment his family and other Japanese experienced during the war. He told of his family being forcibly taken away from Vancouver, their home, to the equivalent of concentration camps inland, as for example in Saskatchewan, to minimize the risk of them aiding and abetting any possible Japanese invasion. One day we received a 1-5 (urgent call) from the third floor. A patient had died and we found Suki on the bed vigorously performing futile external cardiac massage. It took some time for us to convince Suki that his effort was in vain. This was the first patient he had lost and he was duly disturbed.

My first patient death was also very disturbing. I did a pre-op exam one night on an attractive young lass who was going for biopsy of a breast lump the following morning. I did the mandatory complete exam including extensive breast palpation. She followed me intently and at the end she asked "What do you think, doctor? Will I be okay?" I sat on her bed, held her hand, looked into her eyes and assured her as much as I could that based on my examination, the lump seemed to be benign and I was confident that the biopsy would demonstrate that. The following morning, at breakfast before scrubbing up to assist in the operating room, I glanced through the window and saw something white falling down. It was my patient, wrapped in her bed sheet, who had jumped to her death from the sixth floor window of her room. I was shocked and overcome with a feeling of guilt. If only I had been more persuasive about the benign appearance of the lump . . . I vowed never to be flippant about potentially disastrous medical outcomes.

I kept my room above the laundry, shared with a strange intern from Ireland named Dennis. He kept me awake on several nights recalling in agonizing detail the exact, date, time and place of many injustices carried out on the Irish by the "brutal British". He was obviously upset by them and many other happenings. He was skilled in trauma surgery as shown by his performance in the outpatient emergency when the RTAs (road traffic accidents) arrived. Dennis awoke me one night by screaming and shouting "Turn it off, turn it off". I awoke and asked him what the matter was. He said "Look, it's coming towards me". He was pointing at the large, brightly lit cross on the nearby shrine of Brother Andre, the now-sainted Saint Andre who worked so many miracles in Montreal.

Our room opened onto the staff common room and we often spent enjoyable hours having a cold beer after our long work hours. When the fridge was prematurely empty of its precious beer cargo, we immediately solved the problem by phoning Andre the ambulance driver, who promptly arrived to take one of us to the nearest "blind pig" to purchase our illicit alcohol. I would often accompany him on these "emergencies". The siren would blare as the ambulance deftly found its way through various Montreal East addresses where we purchased our booze at exorbitant prices.

Christmas was our most exciting time. We got an abundance of gifts from the patients, office administration and mostly from attending staff. They resulted in an enormous cache of well-earned alcohol, which piled up on the common room table. Our chief resident noted this and challenged us to find a solution to this much-anticipated and ever-expanding pile of booze. "Nicely, Nicely," as we called our chief, summoned a general intern staff meeting and told us to decide the fate of our booze. After a short discussion we agreed that we would take a majority vote whenever possible to reach agreement. As the meeting was drawing to a close I declared, "Well, we are all here now, so why don't we get to work and attack the booze right now." Much vocal acknowledgement pursued and a few hours later the entire cache was demolished as was the majority of our intern staff except for the "on guard" doctors who had been previously identified and ordered to abstain.

MARGARET

My rotation internship included a surgical attachment. The night before I started it I developed a horrible sore throat with a high fever and I reported to the outpatient department. The duty doctor took a look at my pus-covered tonsils, diagnosed a strep throat and ordered a penicillin injection. I was admitted to a ward and shortly after a beautiful nurse arrived with the injection. She asked me if I was allergic to penicillin. I said I was not sure. She then gave me a skin test for penicillin allergy. After one hour she read the test and it was red and swollen. The attending doctor declared me penicillin sensitive and changed the antibiotic. The nurse kindly informed me of this and brought a cold cloth for my forehead and a new antibiotic. I saw the kindness in her actions and her beautiful face and went off to sleep. That wiped me out of my surgical rotation so after my recovery I spent extra time in the outpatient department.

St Mary's was one of the hospitals closest to the infamous Decarie Boulevard, one of the main arteries to northern Quebec via the Laurentians. It was notorious for its traffic crashes so our out-patient department received a steady stream of victims. One night the screaming ambulance deposited a man injured in an auto crash who was bleeding profusely. We quickly proceeded to stabilize him and to carry out the necessary life-saving procedures. I was shocked by his mangled, crushed lower limbs and doubted if they were salvageable. In the midst of our frantic efforts I saw a nurse at the table bending over and gently wiping his forehead, whispering in his ear, "You are going to be OK". I looked at her and it was the same nurse who so kindly looked after me in the ward. I decided to find out more about her and to try to get to know her.

I learned that her name was Margaret Morrison and she was the acting night supervisor. She was a St Mary's nursing school graduate and she had just returned from nursing in California. The rumour was that she returned to enter a religious order as a nursing nun. Winter was an exciting time and the interns decided to jointly rent a cottage in the Laurentians so we could enjoy skiing weekends whenever possible. I went along with this idea even though I did not ski.

At New Year's we decided to have a big party at the cottage where we would invite a partner and spend the two nights. I eventually summoned up the courage to ask Morrison to come and she readily agreed. The weekend was a toxic one with much booze flowing. We climaxed our New Year's Eve party in the early morning. One of our most inebriated interns, an American resident older than the rest of us, played his banjo as we waved sparklers outside the church after New Year's mass and sang:

> It's a wonderful night for singing
>
> Out on old Waikiki Bay
>
> And the hula hips are swinging
>
> In the trim Hawaiian way

And I'm looking for some nookie now

Some nookie, nookie, nookie, nookie, now *(ad nauseum)*

The girls, who were in a separate cottage, were not impressed by our drunken behaviour. Morrison was kind to me and gently cradled my head on her shoulder as we drove back to Montreal. Over the next few weeks I managed to draw close to her. She lived in Notre Dame de Grace and I offered to drive her home after her 11 pm night duty. She invited me into her home and introduced me to her mom and sister Helen who readily made me a BLT sandwich before I fell asleep on the couch. The nightly rides home inevitably led to some pretty close encounters in the car.

I was convinced that Morrison was the woman for me. I just couldn't see life without her love, kindness and beauty. I asked her to marry me and she willingly agreed. Her mother and sister were also in agreement. "Margaret is a good cook, you know," her sister Helen would often remind me.

I announced our future nuptial plans to my fellow interns. These plans were greeted with a good deal of mockery and disdain: "How can you do this to Morrison!" Johnny M demanded. "She is a good woman and you are a Jamaican bum." The St Mary's Catholic hierarchy were also upset at this proposed marriage. The sisters were distressed by the possible loss of one of their novices.

A pleasant surprise came about a week after the announcement. The chief of surgery was a fun-loving loud-mouthed, skilled Irish surgeon called Dr O'Neil.

He thought nothing of giving us a sharp knock on our knuckles with whatever instrument came to hand as we fell asleep under his axilla while retracting the liver for a gall-bladder removal. Once after a particularly exhausting night in the OR when we were in the dressing room, he asked me, "Forbes, I hear that you are going to marry Morrison."

"Yes," I said, anxiously waiting for the worst.

"Do you love her?" he asked.

"I love her very much, sir," I said honestly.

"Well," he said, "we are going to have a party!" His "cottage" in the Laurentians was a vast exotic mansion and the party was a blast. Much whiskey and Jamaican rum, Irish dancing and Jamaican reggae were intermixed with great success.

The wedding was at a nearby Catholic church at Cotes de Nieges. I gladly underwent the mandatory Catholic marriage lessons given to me by Father Henry Hall. I promised to bring up our children in the Catholic faith. The wedding itself was a modest affair. I bought a three-piece suit from A Gold, the tailor man, on a six-month never-never plan. My best man was a fellow Jamaican, Ben Thompson, our chief surgical resident, and our ushers were Johnny Martin and other fellow McGill graduate interns. Our wedding dinner was at a middle-income hotel in a seedy part of Montreal. Margaret's mother and sisters were there as were our workmates. Margaret's father and brothers refused to attend as they disapproved of the wedding of their beloved Margaret to a black man. We both had the weekend off so we decided to go to an inn in the Laurentians for our two-day honeymoon.

We left the hotel and were driving up Decarie Boulevard when a driver, who obviously had had more to drink than I did, cut me off, causing me to exit the Boulevard sharply. I quickly caught up to him and cut him off. I came out of my car and proceeded to verbally abuse him in the best Canadian and Jamaican curse words I could muster. He sheepishly apologized and I returned to my car. "I have never seen you like this," Margaret moaned. "I'm not sure that I want this kind of a man for my husband." I was shocked and I apologized profusely but it certainly affected our honeymoon. I had never slept in pajamas but I thought it prudent to buy a pair for my honeymoon. I put them on as I went to bed and Margaret appeared in a beautiful nightgown. We had a night of ecstasy and that was the last time I have ever worn pajamas.

Our wedding was in May and my internship was due to end in June. My friend Johnny Martin was also preparing to leave St Mary's. He was returning to Ethiopia to be with his family. He and Rose prepared to leave their place in Montreal to spend time in Washington before returning to Ethiopia. They offered us their apartment in Cotes de Nieges, so that was our first marital home.

We returned from our honeymoon on Sunday night, tired and very much in love. I opened a bottle of wine and we lay down on the carpet in the living room. I found a record to play. It was Mendelssohn's piano concerto in E minor No. 4. We held each other closely and fell asleep. To this day that music is of great value to us, bringing back memories of wonderful times spent closely together.

We were both on duty at 8 am Monday morning so it was early rising, showers, and Margaret proceeded to make breakfast. I donned my hospital whites and came to the kitchen while Margaret went to put on her crisp nurse's uniform. I was overwhelmed by the smell and smoke—burnt toast and burnt bacon. Our first breakfast. I recalled the boasts of her sister Helen, "Margaret can cook, you know". Over the years Margaret has learned to cook, mostly to teach the cooks we had in Africa to prepare the dishes that her mother used to make. But to this day I still do the lion's share of the cooking in our home.

At the end of my internship year I had to sit for the most onerous of examinations—the registration examination for the College of Physicians and Surgeons of Quebec. To return to writing exams after we had just finished eight years of perpetual exams was horrible punishment. A group of us studied together into the long hours of the night. Fortunately, we all passed. June came and we prepared to step out into the cold hard world.

Chapter Nine

BACK TO THE RCAMC

I had to pay back the years for which I was subsidized by the Army. I was ordered to report to camp Petawawa on the first of July 1956. Margaret had given me the news of her pregnancy and we eagerly anticipated the arrival of our first born. In preparation for the trip to Petawawa I thought it best to buy a stronger and more reliable car than the aging Mercury, which was on its last legs. I scouted the car lots and found one on Sherbrooke Street that promoted a beautiful-looking Buick. It was on the *place d'honneur* on a stand under bright lights. The salesman pointed out its wonderful features and assured us that it was a "steal at a bargain price". I hurried home and brought Margaret to see it. She was duly impressed so I bought it. I proudly drove it around the hospital to show it (and me) off.

July came and we packed up what few belongings we had and headed to Petawawa Military Hospital—my first post as a real doctor. Marg and I drove the long scenic drive up through the Ottawa Valley through Renfrew and Pembroke to our allotted home in the PMQs (private married quarters) in Camp Petawawa. We settled in quickly with help from a friendly couple across the street. We also made friends with neighbours nearby. One was an Englishman and ex-Indian Army officer, a chef of the Service Corps. He was a pompous man who eagerly tried to enlist me into his cadre of "real English", whose duty it was to teach the unruly Canadians proper customs, dress and speech. He wore a monocle which he alternatively screwed into his face or let drop in surprise or disdain by a skillful wiggling of his peri-orbital muscles. Sundays were his special day to shine as he cooked his self-proclaimed world-renowned Bengali curry. He taught me all the secrets of how he did it and I was fortunately able to replicate his recipe many times in neo-colonial Africa. My son Carl has taken this over from me and his Bengali chicken curry is now a thing to behold and a joy forever.

Our nemesis in Petawawa was the adjutant of the hospital. The commanding officer, Major Harrison, was a non-functioning field officer who was dominated by his wife. She looked like a failed movie star and was devoted to golf while her husband was given the care of her seven children. He had little interest in, and less time to deal with matters regarding the hospital so his adjutant, Lieutenant Harmond (Harry), ran the ship. He delighted in calling me "Officer Cadet Forbes". I reminded him that as a fully qualified doctor I was a captain in the RCAMC. "Not yet, my lad, you have not been gazetted." He meant that my name had not been published in the weekly Canadian government gazette. This also meant that I was in a no-man's land between being an Officer Cadet and a Captain so I was not eligible to be paid a salary.

Our combined St Mary's salaries of intern and nurse quickly ran out and Margaret and I were faced with the frightening actuality. We had no money and no income. I brought this to Harry's attention and he laughed mockingly and said "What are you gonna do?"

Fortunately, at that time I was posted as a regimental medical officer to the Royal Canadian Dragoons. This is the senior cavalry regiment in Canada, a spin-off from the British Dragoons. I quickly learned that it was a prime posting. The regiment was a closely knit group of tank soldiers. Many had served in the Second World War and had fascinating stories about landing in Italy and France. I was welcomed into this family and quickly joined a circle of friends.

The adjutant, a kind tank commander named Vern Lindsey, learned about my financial predicament and released a substantial sum of money from an emergency fund for officers in distress to last me until I was gazetted. Fortunately, the money lasted for two months, until I received my pay plus back allowances. I was then easily able to repay his loan.

I worked diligently at the Petawawa Military Hospital. I remember my first emergency, a call in the early morning to a house near to ours. My sergeant, Barnett, and my provo (police), Sergeant Beard led me into a house where I found a young lady dead. Near her bed was an empty syringe and a bottle of adrenaline. Her husband, a grieving Canadian sergeant, explained that he met his wife while serving in England. She was asthmatic and her doctor told her that since she was going to Canada where medical facilities were limited she should take some adrenaline and if her asthmatic attacks did not stop with the oral Ventolin tablets she should give herself a small dose of adrenalin subcutaneously. The lady gave herself much more than the advised "small dose" and died.

That was my first death on my shift. It upset me a great deal. "What if?" I kept asking myself. I have had a great respect for asthma since then and have witnessed two more deaths from overdose of asthma medication. Later, I taught my students that I was more afraid of asthma medication that of asthmatic attacks.

Chapter Ten

BABIES

My new family of the Royal Canadian Dragoons, the RCDs, provided us with new friends and many happy times. Unfortunately, I became more and more fond of the ever-flowing alcohol. The Friday night happy hour was often the start of a three-day binge. Margaret was growing heavy with child and often declined to accompany me to mess dinners and parties. One morning in early November she awoke me from a drunken slumber to announce "The baby is coming ". As a nurse with extensive obstetrical experience, she was sure to be right. We gathered the prepared baby pack and I drove Margaret in my none-too-reliable Buick to the Pembroke General Hospital about 25 miles away. After her admission to the ward I was told that as it was her first child the baby was not due for awhile. So I left Margaret in the hospital and drove to Pembroke to find an open restaurant where I sat down to breakfast. As I sipped my coffee, the full strength of my impending fatherhood hit me and I prayed to my Lord to give me the strength and guidance that I so much needed. I went back to the hospital to wait it out but on the ward I was greeted by a smiling nurse who announced "It's a girl, they are both fine". I rushed into her room to find Margaret cuddling our first born. I held the baby and kissed her with loving greetings. We spoke briefly about names and decided that we would call her Heather. I went back to camp, announced the good news to my few friends, then went to sleep.

I was awakened by a phone call from Margaret's sister Nicey from Montreal. I gladly announced Marg's delivery but was cut short with the news that Mother Morrison had just had a massive stroke. She insisted that Marg come quickly to Montreal as "Mom was asking for her". My friends came to our rescue. My fellow medical officer, Captain Eric Todd, explained that it was not possible to rush to Montreal in the now-decrepit Buick so I was to take his new Pontiac to complete the trip. Our friend the wife of the HQ commander came to Margaret, who had been quickly released from hospital, and explained how to care for the newborn on the trip. She phoned her sister in Ottawa and instructed us to stop there for rest and refreshment on our way. Nursing sister Captain Zip Sharp showed Margaret the basics of breastfeeding.

I was overwhelmed by this outpouring of love, care and guidance from our newfound friends in this far-away military camp.

It all worked, and we reached Margaret's family in Montreal. There was much consternation about the new baby and our beloved Mom, whose stroke left her confused and without speech. Margaret's sisters Nicey, Pat and Helen took full control of the situation and guided us through this difficult time.

On Sunday, I left to return to my duties. I drove back alone in Eric's superb new Pontiac, keeping awake by blaring the radio, opening the windows and letting the winter air in. I made many weekend trips to Montreal. I would leave on Friday afternoon after duty and speed down the long road to Ottawa. On one of these journeys I was exceeding the 80-mph speed limit when half asleep I noticed the ominous blinking lights of a police car in my rear-view mirror. I pulled over and in despair greeted the circling officer. He shone his flashlight into my face then on my three shoulder pips and said, "What's the hurry, Captain?" I explained with half-truths that my wife was delivering our first baby in Montreal and I wanted to be there to catch it. "That's a good one," he smiled, "but please be careful." I thanked him profusely and drove off slowly. Again, I was overwhelmed by the kindness and understanding from the Canadians whom I met.

Eventually, I brought Marg and Heather back to Petawawa. My regimental life quietened for awhile. Daily as I came home I longed to see my baby and find out what new tricks and fun things she could perform. She was a bright child with advanced development. She quickly learned to smile and at four months developed an enchanting belly laugh when I set about tickling her. Margaret begged me to stop. A favorite trick when she started to crawl was peek-a-boo, when I would scare her as she crawled down the hallway and she would scream and shift into reverse. We enjoyed playing this game immensely and we developed a close bond of love and fun.

One day I came home with the news that I had been chosen to be the medical officer to the Canadian forces in the UN mission in the Egyptian Suez Canal crisis. Margaret was disappointed with my imminent departure and made plans to stay in Montreal. As I was preparing to leave I was called in by the HQ command who informed me that I was not going to Egypt. The powers in Ottawa felt that I looked like an Egyptian so I was not truly able to represent Canada. I accepted this decision, much to Margaret's relief.

Chapter Eleven

WEST GERMANY

Not long after, the good news came. The Royal Canadian Dragoons were chosen to join the NATO British Army of the Rhine in West Germany and I was to proceed there with the regiment. Margaret and Heather were to come later. By this time we knew that Margaret was again pregnant but we were determined that pregnancy would not prevent her from coming. I set off on the *Empress of France* from Quebec City in July 1957 to Iserlohn, West Germany. In its usually questionable logic, army headquarters loaded the 900 officers and men of the RCDs into an enormous ship of the Canadian Pacific line together with the wives and children of a rival regiment, the French Canadian Royal 22nd (The Van-doos).

I shared my cabin with a French Canadian padre, Captain Yves Bernier. He and I both suffered from sea sickness, which hit us as we rolled around in the Atlantic on leaving the St Lawrence River. We greeted each morning with spontaneous, almost coordinated vomiting sessions in the toilet and wash basin. Yves would turn to me and order, "Say three Ave Maria's before we die, Colin." The wives and children of the lower ranks confined to the lower decks were in similar bad shape so I set up my own medical inspection room below decks. Fortunately, my ever-present, omniscient, smiling Sergeant Barnett would help me through the sick parade every morning. We managed to keep the families going with anti-emetics and fluids.

The ship's captain called to tell me that the ship's doctor, a Scot called Andy Byrne, had just come down with the Asian flu so could I please look after the ship's crew as well as my military personnel. I had to accept this added responsibility even though I was also suffering from intermittent bouts of motion sickness.

I conducted my sick parades sitting at a desk with a plastic-lined bucket by my side. I would ask, "What's the matter, soldier (or sailor)? "

"I feel sick, sir."

"How do you think I feel," I said as I barfed into my bucket. Gravol, an anti-emetic, and fluids took us across the Atlantic.

The dining room was ominously empty most of the time. One Sunday I decided to go to the church service conducted by the ship's captain. Appropriately the opening hymn was:

> Eternal father, strong to save,
>
> Whose arm doth calm the reckless wave,
>
> Protect us as we cry to thee,
>
> For those in peril on the sea.

The captain had announced to the anxious congregation, "Due to the inclemency of the weather and the motion of the vessel we will remain seated for the singing of the hymns." I cursed British understatement.

At night Padre Bernier and I would take refuge in the first class bar. The bartender, a salty Scot named Alex, informed us, "This is a bad crossing, sirs, and they don't call this ship the "Drunken Duchess' for nothing." He assured us that the best cure for sea sickness was B&B (brandy and benedictine) which he mixed in copious servings for us and which I still relish in times of stress or worry. One night as I strolled around the deck I spotted a woman leaning over the railing. I asked her what the matter was and she broke into tears, telling me in heavily accented English about the difficulties she was having with her husband and she wondered if it would not be best for her to jump overboard. I gingerly took her arm and assured her that this was not the way. I quickly led her to Padre Bernier who was able to help her.

I woke up one morning and called out to Yves, "How are you this morning?"

"Not bad," he said. "How are you?"

"I feel better," I said.

"You should,' he replied. "We have been docked for five hours in Rotterdam!" We then took the long scenic journey by rail to Iserlohn.

We were ushered into our officers quarters, a huge opulent castle-like building on the outskirts of the village. I was shown my more than adequate private bedroom. It had a cloth hanging over my bed, which rang a bell with which to call for assistance when needed. We learned that this had been the officers barracks of an elite German panzer regiment. We settled in and I quickly set up my medical inspection room. My staff consisted of a driver, Sergeant Barnett, and a batman (orderly), Corporal Brighter, who was an ex-Nazi soldier, and ever-changing privates. We found a suitable building in the camp and renovated it. Sergeant Barnett sheepishly and proudly presented me with a gift. It was a pair of full-length cavalry boots complete with spurs, a relic of the panzer dress uniform. They had been found buried in one of the walls that had been torn down in the renovation. I accepted them and they became an integral part of my number one "blues" regimental uniform.

Our regiment prepared for the arrival of our families. First of all, we had to get our tanks into place. This was a major operation, sending all that hardware from Canada by ship and rail. The tanks eventually arrived at the Iserlohn rail station and were skillfully unloaded and driven through the narrow cobblestone streets of the ancient village to our barracks. Tank crews feel most at home in their tanks and this journey gave the entire regiment a great emotional boost. Not unexpectedly, HQ were presented with a bill from the township of Hemer-Iserlohn for a substantial amount of deutschmarks. It was the charge for damage done by the rumbling of our tanks down their streets; a collection of slightly damaged Hummel figurines were presented as evidence.

The townspeople were welcoming to us, especially when we set up our grocery store—the Maple Leaf Services, stocked with ample supplies of much-appreciated Canadian food such as maple syrup, Bic pickles, Canadian bacon and hotdogs. By far the most useful was instant coffee, eagerly appreciated by our German friends. Indeed, on Friday shopping days many Germans lined the exit to the Maple Leaf Services store, literally begging us for coffee. Our commanding officer ordered me, Barney and Sergeant Bear, the provost sergeant, into his office. He explained that a regiment was as good as its fighting ready men. I knew that, because I had already figured out that at the beginning of any hostilities my regiment of 900 men would only be able to muster one-third (about 300) troops because a third would be irretrievably hung over and a third would be sick with gonorrhea.

The commanding officer, the CO, explained that we were to examine all the bars and whorehouses in the town, choose the ones that would agree to our monitoring services for VD, then list them as being out of bounds, knowing full well that the troops would head straight for them. I was in charge of this dubious assignment, but Sergeant Bear, the largest and most world-wise of us, always led the way into the *gasthofs* and quickly identified the ones we would list.

"Do you want to try any, Captain Forbes?" he would ask.

"Not now," I would reply.

Not to be outdone, the officers had their own night out. I was ordered by the CO to arrange a visit to the infamous German area of ill repute, Saint Pauli in Hamburg. My CO explained that my duty was to inject prophylactic penicillin into any officer including himself who embarked on that ultimate journey.

We decided to commandeer a "deuce and a half"—a two and a half ton troop-carrying vehicle. We went on the long two and a half hour journey by autobahn to Hamburg. I could not believe the sights of St Pauli. Narrow streets with shop windows in which sat beautiful ladies in various stages of undress. The drill was to stop at the shop and negotiate through a half-open window with the beckoning lady.

My CO quickly returned to me as I waited in the truck. "Jam it," he ordered. I loaded my syringe with one million units of penicillin and injected it into the upper-outer quadrant of his right buttock. He quickly buckled his pants and disappeared.

We consumed a great deal of German beer on this expedition then at 2 am we were reminded that we had an early regimental parade so we piled into the truck and sped back to the barracks. I remember looking at the tangled mass of RCD officers on the floor of the truck as I rode in the passenger seat with our newly designated driver, Lt Martin, self-chosen as being the least intoxicated. Soon we were able to see the rays of the morning sun. Our CO extirpated himself from the mess on the floor, looked out and shouted, "We're driving east, asshole, we should be going west!" A quick map check proved that he was right so we did a forbidden U-turn on the autobahn and raced back to barracks. We got there just in time to have a quick shower, get into our battle dress and stumble onto the parade ground. What a woozy parade that was, but, as I was to learn later, the more inebriated an officer is the brighter the step and the smarter the salute until the occasional collapse.

The big day came. Our wives had left Quebec City on the same ship—the *Empress of France* (Drunken Duchess) in which we had crossed. I had already warned Margaret about the ship and advised her how to deal with sea sickness as only I could. We were informed of the arrival date in Rotterdam and I was posted to be the medical officer to meet the vessel and be in charge of the health of the families on the train to Iserlohn.

I was only too pleased to be chosen for this; it would mean that I would have the chance to meet my wife and child and bring them back to our new German home.

We got to Rotterdam and I boarded the ship and was introduced to the ship's doctor, the same Andy Barr who had been so ill on my crossing. He greeted me with the bad news—bad crossing, an outbreak of diarrhoea and vomiting affecting mostly the children, which turned out to be a salmonella outbreak. He quickly assured me that Margaret was one of the few wives who had been able to attend the dining room on a regular basis but our daughter Heather had succumbed to the outbreak. I quickly went to Margaret's cabin and avidly greeted her and Heather. I saw that Margaret was indeed very heavy with child. In the early morning she awoke me with the news that she felt the baby coming. I quickly examined her and indeed she was in labour. I called Dr Barr, who confirmed it and set up an emergency ambulance evacuation. Margaret was strapped to a stretcher and expertly carried to a waiting Royal Army Medical Corps ambulance into which our 11-month-old Heather and I were bundled. We sped over the cobblestone roads to the nearest hospital, the Zuider-Zeekenhuis, with Marg's contractions getting ever stronger.

On arrival at the hospital we were greeted by welcoming and professional nurses. They had been briefed about our arrival and expertly transported us to the delivery room. They quickly and lovingly took Heather from us and cared for her. The senior nurse explained that the hospital rules were that doctors' wives would be delivered by the duty obstetrician, not by midwives. She explained that she had already phoned the specialist but he was slow in coming and suggested that since I was a doctor I would have to deliver the baby myself. I was scared but only too willing to do my best in this emergency. I dutifully washed up while Marg was in the last stages of labour and semi-expertly positioned myself in front of her prepared perineum, waiting to catch my baby. What I did receive was a copious shower of amniotic fluid as her waters broke over my smart officer's uniform complete with Sam Browne belt. The nurse snickered and wiped away excess liquid from my eyes so I could see to guide my first-born son through his mother's birth canal. I did the necessary neonatal examinations while the nurses cared for Margaret. George was 2.6 kilos, just past the official premature weight of 2.5. This was to be of considerable value to me as I explained that my wife had been allowed to travel because she had not yet reached the cut-off time of seven months . . . so he must have been premature. The regimental powers that be quickly let the matter go.

The nurses at the hospital insisted that they take care of Heather that night as I was extremely tired, worn out and stained. They directed me to the nearest hotel to spend the night before returning to Germany the next day. I checked into my room, quickly showered and changed into my spare uniform. It was about 8 pm when I wandered into the grandiose dining hall—just in time to see the waiters packing up the place for the night. The maître d' spotted me and I asked if I was too late to eat. He quickly glanced at my uniform and when he saw the red patch on my arm he shouted "*Kanadische, wilkommen!*" The Canadian forces had played a major role in the liberation of Holland from Nazi rule and this type of recognition was readily awarded to us whenever we were in Holland. He seated me at a sort of head table, brought me a bottle of red wine and ordered an enjoyable dinner. To crown it all, a sleepy-eyed gentleman with quickly donned bow tie and tails staggered over to my table with his violin and asked me if I had any request. I asked him to play "Fascination", an old waltz that Margaret liked to dance to (we still do). Tears came to my eyes as I re-lived the tumultuous events of the day and the incredible kindness of the Dutch, who helped us and ensured the health and safety of my wife, first-born son and his 11-month-old sister.

On the next day, I bade Marg and George goodbye, collected Heather and boarded a train full of RCD wives and children in the long journey to Iserlohn. Poor

Heather was weak and, I realize in retrospect, dangerously dehydrated. I prepared some weakened formula and fed her continually, constantly changing her as her diarrhoea persisted.

We arrived in Iserlohn and I returned to our new home, 69 Brederstrasse Hemer-kreis, Iserlohn. I was met by Ilse, the young *putzfrau* whom I had recently hired to help us in our home. She was surprised to see Heather in her weak condition and quickly boiled us up a German tea that would heal her instantly, she assured me. The next day after copious amounts of my half-strength formula and Ilse's magic tea I could see a definite improvement in Heather. I was forced to leave her with Ilse and attend my regimental medical duties. On return that afternoon I found Heather the happy, healthy child I remembered and Ilse sat me down to copious amounts of soup and *kartoffel* salad. I thanked her profusely and she went upstairs to her quarters as Heather and I spent some happy, quality time together. At the end of the week, I was ordered to return to Rotterdam to bring Marg and George home. I left Heather in Ilse's expert care under the supervision of Allison Withers, the RCD Signals officer's wife, who lived next door.

I found Margaret in good condition, physically and emotionally, happy to see me and to reintroduce our son, who was biting the daylights out of her in the pretense of breastfeeding. We had a joyful reunion. On our return journey to Germany my effusive praise of Ilse and her skills inevitably drew Margaret's suspicion and I had to do some fancy footwork to convince her that I was not involved with Ilse in any other way.

Jealousy was an integral part of Margaret's emotional make-up, as I was to learn repeatedly throughout our long life together. In fact, it fueled some of my later behaviour when I sometimes acted stupidly to prove that "if that's what she wants to think then I will give her reason to think just that". Nuff said! Ilse eventually had to leave as we strongly suspected that the continuous stream of footsteps sounding much like that of RCD soldiers marching up to her room at odd hours of the night made me realize that she was also otherwise gainfully employed.

Marg and I enjoyed our early days in Iserlohn—many regimental dinners and classy military balls. I was enthralled by having such a beautiful, bright Canadian woman as my wife and took every opportunity to show her off. Her charm was also noted by some of the horny young, single tank officers. I often came home to find one of them sitting in my living room being served tea by my wife. As time went by, our closest friends became the Signals officer, Ramsey Withers, and his wife Allison, who also had a young family. Ramsey asked me to be the godfather to Laura, one of his twin girls, and we had appropriate christening and "afters".

Ramsay was an expert logistician, a graduate of Royal Military College and a dedicated Canadian soldier. The RCDs often went on tank manoeuvres. This meant days in the bush driving the tanks over all types of terrain and playing war games. The non-tank officers had to accompany the regiment on these prolonged exercises. The four of us: the padre Jim Johnson, the Signals Officer Ramsay Withers, the paymaster and me (the Regimental Medical Officer) spent hours and days in a jeep following the idiotic tanks around, waiting for a crisis. Crises came only sporadically so the rest of the time, to prevent death from boredom, the four of us invented a game of "tell the best dirty joke". Mine invariably won. Here's one of them:

An old RCD officer, recently widowed, was urged by his daughter to leave his home of 40 years and spend his twilight days in a retirement complex, a luxurious set of cottages in a beautiful surrounding. The major spent about a year there, quietly sitting in his rocking chair and eating the always healthy prepared meals brought to him. One day, in a fit of disgust, he painted a sign and stuck it outside his cottage. It read "Sex available here, $1 for the bed and 25 cents on the floor". He went into his cottage and continued rocking in his chair until a few hours later a lovely old lady in a gingham dress and a flowered hat knocked on his door. He quickly opened it, saw the lovely old lady and said "Come right in". She shuffled in and he asked, "What do you want?"

She replied, "I saw your sign."

"You want sex?" he barked.

"Yes," she sheepishly replied.

"OK," he shouted. She dug deeply into her brassiere, took out a dollar bill and handed it nervously to him.

"OK," he barked, "get up on the bed!"

"No," she said, "I want four on the floor."

This invariably brought the jeep shaking with laughter, leaving me very proud of my sit-down comic capabilities. After awhile inevitably we ran out of jokes and had to recycle them. We eventually found it easier to number our jokes, then we'd merely just shout the number: "Say 47!"

Then a prompt "RCD widower" and we would all burst out laughing.

Once the regiment took an extra long trip with the tanks to a part of West Germany called Falling Bostock, otherwise known to us as "effing B". We were told that this was where Hitler used to come to watch his panzer divisions fire their guns. At this time we were on manoeuvres with an English cavalry regiment, the Royals, after which the RCDs were named. The Brits always considered themselves more than a cut above us, so one of our officers decided to play a trick on them. They decided to pretend that I was the "coloured" bartender in the mess and they would treat me as they imagined the Brits would treat the coloured in their ranks.

I was set up behind its bar; on drinks parade before and after dinner, my friends came to me and shouted, "Hey boy, the usual!"

"Isn't he so clumsy?" "Respect your visiting officers, boy!" The Brits were appalled as I dutifully and gleefully played my part.

One of Ramsay Withers's greatest accomplishments was to figure out how to get the most legitimate (or near so) holidays. When we considered Canadian holidays, German holidays and special holidays such as those granted by the royal family on their incessant visits, we invariably were able to set up a two-week break every three or four months. Ramsay then planned our many visits to various European countries, which took us to Italy, Spain, France, Belgium and repeatedly to Holland. We dutifully visited the suggested museums, cathedrals, palaces and other places of supposed interest. I remember in Paris joining a tour group led by a stout middle-aged lady who thought she spoke English. "Follow my red umbrella," she sternly instructed—and we did so all through the Notre Dame cathedral. In Rome, we were enthralled by the historic sites.

Once in Greece we managed to link up with our hippie friends Max and Eileen from Montreal. Max had been one of my students at McGill, a brilliant student who was deeply involved in the anti-Vietnam war movement. His wife had been my lab assistant while I was doing post-graduate research at the Montreal Children's Hospital. We were testing an anti-asthmatic drug, one of the many to emerge at that time. The test consisted of giving the child two puffs of the adrenogenic mixture, wait five minutes then have the child exhale forcibly into an expiratory flow meter. The success of the drug compared with the results obtained by those in the placebo group established the usefulness, safety and acceptance of the drug. Little did I realize how the results could be affected so greatly by the instructions given to the child. With the placebo, my assistant Eileen would say quietly, "Blow blow blow" and measure the forced expiratory volume. When measuring the effect of the test drugs Eileen would demonstrate with exaggerated contortions and shout "BLOW BLOW BLOW!" then whisper "you little bastard". Of course the results demonstrated a greater effect with the test drug.

Eileen also had a part-time job as a go-go dancer in a night club, performing suggestive movements in a plexiglass cage. She made more money than her husband. Max then decided, just after his graduation, to drop out of medicine, travel the world and learn to play the guitar and sing like his friend Leonard Cohen. That's how we met up in Greece.

Inevitably, Marg announced one day that she was again pregnant and expertly, as usual, she produced our third child, Patricia, born in the British Military Hospital in Iserlohn, delivered by our good friend and neighbour Major Athol Roberts from Prince Edward Island.

That did not stop us from our European travels. As soon as Marg finished the mandatory four-month breastfeeding time we were off again. I clearly remember pushing Pat in the pram and holding onto Heather and George as we went shopping in nearby Dusseldorf. In a large department store I was buying a necklace for Margaret. We looked in the mirror and to our surprise it seemed as if the entire store was looking at us. I heard remarks such as "*So junge mensh und so fiele kindern* (such young people and so many children)" and "*Er ist ein swanzanaegger* (he is a black man)." One of them asked permission to touch my skin to see if it was really black.

###Our many trans-European trips were made possible by the kindness and insistence of our neighbour Frau Weineger. She was an efficient, caring, middle-aged woman, whose husband admitted to having been a Nazi army officer. He and I spent many nights together demolishing bottles of expensive brandy, purchased duty free from the British NAAFI stores. She lovingly cared for our children, helped by our hired *putzfrau* while we were away.

The time came when our term of duty was imminent. One night while in bed reading a British medical journal,

I showed Marg an advertisement for Senior House Officer for duties at the Hospital for Sick Children, Great Ormond Street, London, England. "Hey," I shouted to her, "that's where Major Roy came from." Alan Roy was my senior pediatrician at BMH Iserlohn. He first introduced me to hospital pediatrics and I learned a great deal from him. Margaret immediately jumped at the prospect of my obtaining such a valuable position, so I dutifully applied. I received an invitation to come to London for a formal job interview. Major Roy told me that Great Ormond Street was the best children's hospital in the British Empire and he would recommend me highly. I excitedly prepared to travel to London for the interview. I travelled to the Hook of Holland to sail to Harwich for my trip. That night at the Hook, I walked up and down the boardwalk, wondering why there was such excitement. The answer soon became evident—it was the final of the World Cup series, Germany vs Holland. TV was in its infancy and every shop window was showing the game. Inquisitively, I peaked over shoulders in town to see Holland score the winning goal.

On arrival in London, I reported to Great Ormond Street dressed in my full army officer's uniform. I stepped into the lobby and reported to a large, officious-looking commissioner at the desk with his name proudly presented—S.M. Pusey. He looked, spoke and acted like a British sergeant major. "How can I help you, captain?" he asked. I explained that I was here for my interview for the post of Senior House Officer. "OK Guv!" he winked. "Just wait over there", pointing to a small room already occupied by three other applicants. All were post-graduates with MRCP degrees (Member of the Royal College of Physicians). One was a beautiful Indian lady in a stunning, midriff-revealing sari and the other two were intense-looking young Englishmen. They looked at my uniform and asked me if I had an MRCP. To their relief I admitted that I had not, but as a Canadian we obtained our degrees (FRCP) at the end of our post-graduate training. They scoffed at that and at me. I felt defeated. I was second to be called by Mr Pusey. I entered a large hallowed hall lined with pictures of famous British pediatricians and occupied by a group of sleepy-looking professors sitting around a large table. I entered and a few of them appeared to wake up. Not knowing what to do, I resorted, as an army officer, to do what was second nature to me. I came sharply to attention and saluted smartly, the open-handed British way. That awakened all of them and I heard a loud voice, "The red patch—you're a Canadian." I explained my posting in Germany with the NATO forces.

"Well," said Professor Reginald Bonham-Carter, "I haven't seen that red patch in years." I was then excused to wait in another room until Pusey returned to announce that I had been awarded the post.

I was ecstatic and quickly returned to Iserlohn to give Margaret the good news. She was overjoyed as to her it meant deliverance from the Canadian Army and my dangerous battle with alcoholism. We then sat down to decide what to do with our family. We could not afford to live in London so we decided that Margaret, Heather, George and Patricia would go to my home in Jamaica while I did post-graduate training in Great Ormond Street. My family in Jamaica said that they would be happy to have Marg and our children so we hurriedly packed them off by air to Kingston, Jamaica. I saw Margaret off with our three little children, including Pat in her arms as she had a cast on one foot to treat an early club foot. I was overwhelmed with sadness, fear and admiration for my dear wife, who was undertaking this daunting journey alone. Left alone, I busied myself with exiting the Canadian Army in West Germany and preparing myself for my new post-graduate training in England. I took delivery of the Borgward car that we decided to buy. For all our years in West Germany we had driven the second-hand "Hitler" Mercedes that had been forcibly sold to us by Villi, the self-appointed regimental used car dealer. Like others of his ilk he was excessively friendly and willing to give advice on many matters of life in Germany.

My RCAMC replacement in Iserlohn was a friendly, smiling doctor from the Maritimes. His family had arrived also and he was anxious to settle in. I could honestly recommend that he buy my Mercedes, which had taken us all over Europe with no real problems. He willingly agreed and I later heard that he also had had trouble-free driving for three years and then sold it for a handsome profit. Villi had enthusiastically recommended that we purchase a new car—the Borgward, produced in Hamburg by a family business that proudly boasted their impeccable services over the years. The price was reasonable but one of the conditions of purchase was that I would have to go to the factory to take possession. I willingly did this. On arrival in Hamburg, I realized that this was a two-way affair. I took an inspection tour of the factory and they inspected me to see if I was worthy of owning their renowned vehicle. I gave the balance of payment and left on my long drive back to Iserlohn.

In Germany, to this day, there is no speed limit on the super highway that Hitler built, the autobahn, so I tried out my new car to the fullest and was very satisfied. About half-way home, I was tired and stopped at one of the many roadhouses on the autobahn. I checked into my room, had a great meal and went to bed. The next morning at breakfast I noticed some rather charming ladies examining my car. When I prepared for departure one of them approached me and asked me where I was going. I told her Iserlohn and she quickly asked me for a ride. I went back to the desk and was warned by the clerk not to get mixed up with those "Autobahn Mollies" who were whores and did more than one naughty thing to unsuspecting customers. My new car was the envy of my fellow officers and we took it on some wild rides on the autobahn. Eventually it was time to leave West Germany for England. The RCDs threw a party for me, the details of which I cannot remember. They gave me a bronze artillery piece and a horse blanket, which I still cherish.

Chapter Twelve

ENGLAND

The drive to England was an exciting one, speeding my new car through unfamiliar territory in North Rhine Westphalia and then Holland. At the Hook I again boarded a huge ferry to Harwich. I settled in to my cabin but was soon awakened by a seaman who shouted excitedly, "Doctor, come quickly." I dashed out and followed him into the crew quarters in the bowels of the ship. There I saw a seaman lying in his bed with a knife thrust through his chest and copious amounts of blood drained from his heart. He had been dead for some time so I did the usual pronouncement of death and covered him up. By that time many of the crew had gathered around and one of them told me that the captain would like to see me. On entry to his cabin I was greeted by a tall, bronzed, uniformed man with blond hair. "My manifest," he said, "tells me that you are Captain Forbes, RCAMC." Then he broke into an unmistakably Cayman Island dialect and shouted "Co-lin, don't you remember me? I'm Trevor Bodden. We were at Wolmer's together. Sit down and have some Captain Morgan, man!" It is said that long ago a Scottish ship was wrecked off the coast of the Cayman Islands and its passengers settled there. At one time it seemed that every second person in those islands was named Bodden and they all spoke with an unmistakable accent. We polished off the bottle of Jamaican rum and I stumbled back to my cabin to finish the rest of the journey.

At Harwich, I got out my Tour-Europa guide and went on my way to Great Ormond Street. I quickly settled into my new home, a staff residence attached to the hospital. I had a small room with a bed and a desk, where I would spend the next year of my life. I unpacked and set up a picture of Margaret and my three children on my desk. I was to kiss that picture tearfully every night.

Early the next morning I reported to the office and was told that I had been allocated to ward 2–C&D to serve as a "houseman" to Sir Wilfred Sheldon and Dr Phillip Evans. This turned out to be the plum posting for housemen. Sir Wilfred was the Queen's pediatrician and Dr Evans was a brilliant, kind neurology-oriented pediatrician. I reported on my ward in my starched white uniform and was greeted by a beautiful sparkly-eyed nurse who introduced herself as Staff Hardisty. She led me to the nurse in charge, Sister Leavesly, who was dressed in earlier-century uniform with a starched cap, high-collared pleated blouse and high boots. Sister Leavesly looked me up and down and curtly outlined my duties and the hours of the two consultant staff rounds. Sir Wilfred's rounds were on Thursday mornings and we had to be fully prepared for them. I would present all the sick children to him with their full medical history, our clinical findings, my working diagnosis, the investigations we ordered, their results, my treatment and the progress of the child. Sir Wilfred would listen more or less intently, examine the child, make a few observations and suggestions, then we would move on. We would also be treated to a few smart-ass remarks by Dr Mike Simkiss, the resident assistant physician (RAP) and Dr Tom McKendrick, the next senior on the totem pole.

The rounds also attracted a large body of postgraduate pediatricians in training. Many were foreigners from Africa or India. I remember one day Dr Simkiss was late to join the round and he edged his way through this throng of dark-skinned doctors up to Sir Wilfred, who reached over, held out his hand to Simkiss and said "Dr Livingston, I presume". Not everyone laughed. After these rounds we returned to the doctors' room where Sister Leavesly and the staff nurses busied themselves serving us tea and cucumber or Marmite sandwiches. Sister always confronted Sir Wilfred with reminders such as that today was his day to attend to the Queen's children at Buckingham Palace. She would straighten his tie and pin a fresh rose on his lapel, generally making him look and feel very important. We were all impressed and bathed in the reflective glory of this great man.

Once, I made a brilliant diagnosis on a young girl who had intractable abdominal pain. After making a complete work-up I decided that she had primary hyper-parathyroidism. Proudly I presented this child to Sir Wilfred. He said "Do you know how many children have been diagnosed with this disease in England?" I told him that I did not know. "One," he said, "and I was the doctor who reported it." I was overwhelmed. "Make sure you publish this, Forbes," he said. I did, with him as the senior author, as usual.

I had exciting times at Great Ormond Street, not the least of which were my relationships with the English nurses. Many were impressed by my new car and begged me to take them for a ride. This was difficult as I only had Thursday night and Friday mornings officially off. At New Year, one particularly insistent nurse introduced herself as April Mayhew (or call me April May June) and convinced me that we should spend New Year's Eve in Trafalgar Square—"everyone in London will be there," she explained. I drove down, parked my car a long distance away and joined an enormous throng of loud, drunken bodies counting down the seconds to midnight then hugging and kissing everyone in reach. That was a memorable night.

Occasionally on Thursday nights I escaped from the hospital and walked the short distance to the theatres of the West End. There I was to see many wonderful plays and musicals. I got a single seat in the front row at *My Fair Lady* and heard Rex Harrison and Julie Andrews do their wonderful performance. I also heard Eartha Kitt's marvelous show highlighted by "Fever". After one of these performances I was walking on Oxford Street when I saw a sign saying Ronnie Scott's Nightclub. I had heard about this West Indian who played great Caribbean music so I dashed in, sat down and ordered a beer—warm, of course. After awhile a waiter approached and gave me a generous slug of Jamaican rum. I explained that I could not afford this and he winked at me and whispered "It's OK, Guv, it's on the house". I acknowledged the gift and guzzled it down.

As my term as Senior House Officer at Great Ormond Street was finishing, I noticed that Sir Wilfred and Phillip Evans seemed to be more friendly to me. Phillip asked me what my plans were and I told him that I would leave the army and return to Montreal to continue my post-graduate training in pediatrics at McGill. He advised me to stay another six months at Great Ormond Street and carry on some research for him on strokes in children. He explained that I could continue my salary with a research grant he had. He kindly took me out to lunch at a fancy restaurant.

Sir Wilfred explained that he was having a big party at this house and he invited me to come. I gladly accepted but was ordered, "Bring your bongos, Forbes, you shall play them for us." It was a real high society affair with many upper-class titled folk, mostly doctors. I shyly crept in and settled into a corner of the great hall of his residence with my lonely set of bongos. Sir Wilfred eventually announced me as a great Jamaican doctor who would perform on the drums. Loosened up by copious quantities of Jamaican rum I took centre stage, clasped the bongos between my legs and sang "Day-O". Soon I had the entire party joining in many calypsos including "Jamaica Farewell" and "Man Smarter".

It was Christmas time and I had no idea about the importance of this to an English hospital. Great Ormond Street had a time-honoured Christmas party. In fact a great English writer had donated the entire proceeds of *Peter Pan* to this hospital. The party was often attended by royalty and the entire evening was devoted to songs and skits taking the mickey out of the senior staff, and general levity. I was asked—ordered—by Mike Simkiss to get something Jamaican going. Many of the cleaning and general service staff of the hospital were Jamaicans so I approached them about providing these fine English folk with some good Jamaican fun. They willingly agreed. I wrote a substantial calypso and we spent many nights practising it. We agreed on our dress code—Jamaican style dresses and overalls, panama hats and lots of hip swaying. It all sounded great in practice and I was ever so confident that it would be well received. On the big night the word went around that Princess Alice (the Queen's aunt) would be attending. I was busy setting up the props in the large auditorium when a timid Jamaican lady whom I recognized as a worker in the laundry room sheepishly approached me. She explained that she was asked by the entire Jamaican cast to tell me that they could not perform our Jamaican songs before such an important crowd including the aunt of "Missis Queen". I explained that I completely understood and that I myself was beginning to have more than butterflies in my stomach and lower down in the GI tract, but that as seasoned actors, "the show must go on". The emissary then shyly suggested "Maybe we could get a *likkle sumfin* to give us strength". I immediately recognized her meaning; I told her to get the group together and I would be right back. I dashed upstairs to my room and grabbed one of the many bottles of Jamaican rum that I had received for Christmas. I hurried down, brandishing it with much applause as we passed it around. The show was a resounding success and Princess Alice thanked me for such an enjoyable evening. The next morning I was approached by the professor of pediatrics, Dr Bernard Schlesinger, who explained that his son was a prominent movie producer and when he heard of our show he wanted to meet me.

That afternoon I met with Peter Schlesinger, later to be a great British film producer, and he asked me to write a song for a film that he was making about Jamaican migration to England. I quickly wrote a calypso called "Jamaican Memories". We met again the next day with a talented musician who read my script then sat at the piano and transformed it into the same song I had in mind when writing it. I later learned that the movie won some great prizes and my song was honoured as the best. I received a cheque for 25 pounds for this, so I was able to add that amount to my monthly payments to my wife in Jamaica.

All good things must come to an end, so inevitably I prepared for my departure from England. There was much homework to be done as technically I was still in the Canadian Army. I had decided to return to McGill to continue my post-graduate studies in pediatrics. I reported to the Canadian Army Liaison Establishment (CALE) in the middle of London. I explained my plans and the duty officer did the requisite and returned with my honourable discharge papers. He asked me if I was sure that I wanted to leave the Army and when I assured him that I did he explained, "Well Captain Forbes, we have just received our instructions about your promotion to Major with its pay increase, also a newly established professional pay scale and family allowance increases. All of this means that you would be earning twice as much as you do now. Think about that!." I did just that for about five minutes then I took two deep breaths and said "Yes sir. I have to return to McGill for my post-graduate studies." I collected the necessary papers and funds and bade the Canadian Army goodbye.

Chapter Thirteen

RETURN TO CANADA

My return to Canada by ship was arranged by the Army with the usual officer's first-class passage. I packed up my meagre belongings and the little gifts I was taking back to my family and made plans to leave on the *Empress of France* from Southampton to Montreal. I planned to drive my Borgward to the ship to be loaded. The night before, I sat having a lonely last meal in the dining room when I was approached by the homely Lady Almoner, the social worker who had helped me so much with many of my patients who needed various types of financial and family care. Sir Wilfred was very much aware of the effects of the deprivation of this kind of assistance on the life of a child and he would often turn to me and above the rim of his glasses order, "Call in the Lady Almoner, Forbes". She knew of my imminent departure and offered to put me up at her flat to get a good night's sleep before I left the following morning. I gladly accepted her offer and she cooked a lovely meal served with fine wine and other things.

I had been approached by an Indian senior registrar in ENT who learned that I was going back to the Montreal Children's Hospital. He too had accepted a post-graduate post for training at McGill so we had a common bond. I picked him up and drove to Southampton with him as navigator. His name was Raj Kapoor and we became good friends for the next few years. Once when viewing the GOS resident staff photo hanging on my wall in my office in Nairobi, one of my Indian parents told me that Raj Kapoor was one of India's prominent movie actors. I gained reflective glory in my friendship with such a great Bollywood personality.

MONTREAL

I returned to Montreal in July 1960 and was met by my sisters-in-law Helen and Nicey. They had learned of my plans to reunite with my family in Montreal and they had arranged a rental apartment in a veteran's co-op in Montreal West called Benny Farm. We set about redecorating the attractive little flat with Helen and me doing the painting. Helen was as fond of Molson's beer as I was, so it was a wonder that we did not fall off the ladders. Soon afterwards, we drove to Dorval Airport to welcome my family, who had just flown up from Jamaica. There was an unexpected delay as the Canadian immigration authorities found it difficult to classify my children, one born in Canada, one in Holland and the third in Germany.

At long last I saw Margaret and our three little children coming down the passageway. The kids ran to me, hugged and kissed me while Margaret almost collapsed in relief that her long journey had ended and we were at last together in her home town. The children excitedly started to tell me their stories, all in the broad Jamaican accent that I had almost forgotten and which Margaret could barely understand. "George fall down and juk him eye," Heather explained.

Pat took her thumb out of her mouth long enough to inform me "I love you, daddy."

We piled into our Borgward and drove to our new Canadian home. The children enjoyed themselves until one day they came to tell us that the other children in the playground had told them that they were not welcome as they came from a "nigger family". This hurt us a lot so we immediately made plans to leave this neighbourhood.

I had started my job as chief resident at the Montreal Children's Hospital, first in the outpatient department then in the inpatient. My duties included drawing up duty rosters, overseeing the care given in the out-patient department, arranging the weekly clinical rounds, assisting with the special clinics, writing endless reports on the performance of various interns, and so forth. For all of this I was paid the princely sum of $275 per month.

Our move from Benny Farm was to an upbeat neighbourhood called Hampstead where we rented a downstairs duplex for $250 per month. Fortunately, Margaret quickly secured a post as a senior nurse at St

Mary's hospital, night shifts. I also started to obtain endless part-time jobs to augment our income, allowing us to live more or less comfortably. At one stage, I had four part-time jobs: 1) night duty MD at Dorval Airport, 2) examining officer at the Montreal Army recruiting depot ("Turn your head to the right and cough, soldier" as I poked my finger up his inguinal canal searching for hernias), 3) medical officer for a school board in Quebec and 4) weekend medical officer for the RCAF station hospital at Saint-Jean Quebec.

Putting all these pay cheques together was Margaret's job, so that each month we could pay our rent and on Friday nights, I could load our three children onto a sled and slush through the snow to the nearest Steinberg's store to get our weekly shopping needs. Not long after, Margaret broke the news that she was pregnant again. We were devastated as we were barely able to care for the three children we had. She being a staunch Catholic, there was no option but for us than to go ahead with the pregnancy. Margaret continued to work, bringing in the much-needed funds till one morning in February she awoke me with the news, "I'm in labour!"

I called her sister Pat whose husband Gaston ordered me, "Don't you dare take her in your car. You don't have a heater!" So he came quickly and piled us into his car while aunts looked after the children.

We were ushered into the maternity at St Mary's and I waited in the "agony room" where I chain-smoked in anticipation. After what seemed to be a millennium our beloved obstetrician, a tall gangly gentleman named Dr Graham Bailey, appeared at the door in his stained

OR gown. I jumped up as he said "It's all right, Colin, Marg's fine, you have a boy!. Then as he turned to leave he shouted over his shoulder, "And a girl!" Then he dashed off. I slumped into the chair in disbelief and instant anxiety. How would I care for two additional babies? I had prepared a nice little crib for one baby and when I returned home I started to convert it into a double. I assured Margaret that all would be well and I held her and my two new children closely, affirming my love for Marg, Judy and Carl.

Those were busy times indeed and we are eternally grateful for Margaret's sisters' help in many ways. One morning after a particularly difficult night shift, I was in the cafeteria grabbing a cup of coffee when one of the staff pediatricians, a French Canadian, came over to me and said "I heard of the additions to your family. I won't congratulate you but please take this, you will need it", and he pressed $20 into my hand. I later learned that he had seven children.

The appointed time came, and I was soon to write my final examinations in pediatrics of the Royal College of Physicians of Canada. I had studied hard for them, as hard as I could with endless night duties on top of my regular daytime work. Marg continued her night duties at St Mary's so whenever I could get home, I would care for the children, especially the newborn twins. She breastfed them for as long as she could then gave them bottle feeds. Fortunately, the formula producers were actively promoting a new product and one group supplied us with a year's supply of formula for free. Another company supplied us with a bountiful amount of disposable diapers. One night, nearing my finals, I desperately had to get through the final chapters of *Nelson's Pediatrics*. The twins had to be fed so I made up the required formula and took a twin in each elbow, crossing my hands to feed them both. I had to prop my heavy textbook in front of me on a makeshift pedestal and I turned the pages with my tongue.

The written final went well and I was invited to Toronto for the oral exams. I was approached by Dr Dick Goldbloom, one of our renowned Montreal pediatricians, who told me that he was going to be one of the examiners in Toronto. He earnestly advised me, "I know how you feel, Colin, but Toronto is an uptight city and I am not sure how they will take to your beard, so my advice is take it off." I thanked him and the next morning I shaved off half of my chin beard and appeared at breakfast. Margaret burst into laughter in disbelief. "You're not going like that, are you?" I then shaved completely and trotted off to Toronto. That is the last time I have been beardless. Fortunately, luck was on my side and I was able to do very well in my orals so I was invited to a special room for the successful ones and we were given a glass of wine and welcomed into the Royal College as full-fledged pediatricians.

On my train journey back to Montreal I wondered about the many plans I had made once I became a pediatrician. It had taken me eight post-graduation years. I decided to apply to the pharmaceutical company that had taken much interest in my career. They sponsored a weekend in New York for some residents and nurses, which turned out to be a wild affair. I reported to their office on the high levels of the new towers in Place

Ville-Marie. A warm welcome awaited me and I was led into a huge, tastefully decorated room that had a view of the entire downtown Montreal to the St Lawrence River. "This is your office, Doc" the welcomer told me. "Hope you like it." He explained that I was to become the Canadian image of this powerful American drug company. He began a series of instructions accompanied by appropriate business cards. He gave me one for the hairdresser who would perform the company haircut and possibly cut my beard off. In those days, a beard still bore the hippie image. He also gave me a card for the in-house tailor who would provide me with appropriate suits, ties and shoes. He then dropped the bombshell—my salary was to start at $15,000 per year plus a host of expense goodies. Considering that the most I had ever earned was $5,000 a year, this was a welcome offer.

I rushed home to give Margaret the good news. Disappointingly, she asked me, "Is that really what you want to do?" I realized that I was prostituting myself in order to bring more business into the company. I then began having serious doubts, especially about the "company image" bit.

Chapter Fourteen

OFF TO AFRICA

Previously, I had applied to the Canadian External Aid Department for a post as a pediatrician in Africa. This was a hangover from my days when I wanted to be a medical missionary to serve my poor benighted brothers and sisters in that poverty-stricken continent. I did receive a letter inviting me to Ottawa to discuss the possibility of obtaining such a post. One had just become available as a general duty medical officer in a remote village in the then Tanganyika. I located the country on the map as being on the coast of East Africa and quickly agreed to accept this post. Margaret gladly joined me in the preparations to proceed to Africa. We were helped by Max and Eileen. Max was then very involved in his guitar studies. Eileen and Max took it upon themselves to obtain great bargains in tropical clothing for all our five children. A relative of theirs was in the clothing business so we were urged to buy a heap of clothing deemed necessary at an exaggerated price. As our departure time drew near I prepared myself as best as I could. I bought a book on *Learning Swahili* and I even visited a shop that sold clothing for tall women. Margaret was taller than I was so that impressed me. Many going away parties later we set off for Dar es Salaam. We stopped off in London to bid goodbye to my sister Norma, her new husband, John, and their girls. Fitting seven bodies into a modest home in Hertfordshire was not easy but we made it.

Leaving London we flew in a BOAC Comet first class as per Canadian government regulations of the time. Marg and I got the children all settled. Our twins were two and a half years old and Carl was fascinated by cars. I provided him with a pocketful of toy cars which he manoeuvred over the seats and arm rests and windows of the aircraft for the entire journey with accompanying engine noises. We touched down in Benghazi, Libya, and I got out to breathe in African air for the first time.

TANZANIA

On landing in Nairobi we were met by a Canadian diplomat, who handed us over to the government of Tanzania pediatrician sent to meet us. He was an Indian gentleman decked out in the colonial civil service tropical uniform of the time—all white, starched, short sleeved shirt and shorts, and "safari boots" with knee-length white socks into which were inserted a comb, pen and often a pipe.

His name was Zak Mohammed and he introduced himself as the only pediatrician in East Africa. He had been trained in England and held an MRCP degree from Edinburgh. He explained that once he discovered that I had a pediatric degree he insisted that I do not go to Korogwe village but remain in Dar as his assistant. He explained that he was a consultant because he had an English degree but my Canadian degree only allowed me to practise under his supervision. I countered that this was not so as a Canadian fellowship degree established one as a fully fledged consultant pediatrician, able to practise independently. While driving us from the airport he explained that we were lucky to have come at this time because before independence (a year previously) nonwhites were not allowed to cross Selander Bridge which led to Oyster Bay, the white colonial enclave where we were to live.

My first professional experience in Africa was uncomfortable. Mohammed would change my orders, explaining to the nurses that "This doctor is from Canada and does not know anything about African pediatrics and we must help him." I was put in charge of one of the children's wards in the new Muhimbili Teaching Hospital. At that time all the nurses in charge of wards were English colonial service sisters. Mine was an obnoxiously rude woman who was determined to put me in my place, coarsely interrupting my orders and correcting my notes. "That's h.s. doctor, not QHS," or "That's tds, not tid."

Her assistant was a large Indian nurse whose job it seemed was to grab hold of a poor African mother's wizened breast, squeeze it mockingly and pronounce,

"*Hakuna maziwa hapa* (no milk here), give her the bottle." To give an African village mother a bottle with which to feed her baby is tantamount to giving her a gun to kill the child. Factors such as clean water and the prohibitive cost of the formula, forcing mothers to drastically dilute the feed, militate against the health of the newborn.

I was also put in charge of the pediatric ward at the Infectious Disease Hospital across the road. The wards were divided by diseases: polio, measles, whooping cough and leprosy wards. I made daily rounds there and it was heart wrenching. The measles ward had the most patients and the poor children there suffered distressingly from a combination of pneumonia, gastroenteritis, encephalitis, conjunctivitis, dermatitis and malnutrition. Death came to 30% of the children admitted in this ward, usually in the end from choking. The vocal cords became encrusted with a flaky lining and the child was unable to breathe. This was the effect not only of the measles itself but of the underlying vitamin A deficiency. It was sometimes impossible for me to force a laryngeal tube past the almost closed vocal cords so we often performed emergency throat slitting, aka tracheostomy, in an also often futile attempt to save the poor child's life. The whooping cough ward was worse. The children were convulsed by the classical triad of pertussis—paroxismal cough, whoop and vomit. Nothing seemed to help although we slavishly administered the erythromycin, IV fluids and anti-emetics. The death rate here was 50%. The polio ward was a frightening experience. As most children with paralytic polio disease died quickly we had to take care of the adults.

The prevailing treatment for the adults whose breathing muscles were paralysed was to put them into an ingenious machine, seal it airproof and have it breathe for them by a system of increasing and decreasing pressures. This was the iron lung, a fore-runner to the life-saving ICU respiratory assisting devices of today. I was touched by the six or more, mostly male, heads poking out of these machines every morning as I made rounds. Most of them were in incredibly good humour in a bizarre sort of way. They would try to smile and those who could talk would try to crack a joke. "Gin and tonic today, Doc." We dutifully fed them through their nasal intro-gastric tube. Incredibly, some of them survived and were able to go home with only residual limb paralysis.

All this was professionally and emotionally draining on me, coming from my first world training and experience. I had to diligently catch up on the proper management of these diseases. This I did with regular reviews of the *Manson Barr Tropical Medicine* bible plus my ever-present *Nelson's Pediatrics*.

My family suffered. Here we were in an old colonial government house called a PWD (public works department) house in a civil service enclave in Oyster Bay.

Our kids on the beach at Oyster Bay.

Fortunately we were a mere block away from the Indian Ocean, and whenever I could I would take my family to the beach to enjoy the warm water and the white sands. In true colonial fashion I went home for lunch every day. One particularly hot day I was driving to my new home along a still unfamiliar road when I was abruptly jarred by the sight of an enormous snake which took up the entire width of the road as it was crossing in front of me. My heart pounded as I slowed down to allow it to cross and I slowly proceeded to my home. I was shocked to realize that it had just exited my garden as I turned into my driveway to be greeted by five mostly naked, barefooted children shouting "Daddy, daddy!" and jumping onto my lap. I told Margaret and she then related all the snake stories that were the favourites of the morning expatriate wives' coffee parties which she attended for awhile.

The colonial habit was to eat a small lunch and to rest after. I quickly adjusted to this routine and the rest became an important part of my Dar es Salaam life. No napping in a chair for me. I undressed completely, covered myself with a thin sheet and went to my bed directly under the omnipresent ceiling fans for at least one hour. I would then take a quick shower and return to my work at the hospital. This mid-day siesta became a part of my life and it has been so to this day. I strongly recommend it as a survival tactic.

One Sunday as I was having my afternoon rest I was awakened by a Land Rover screaming to a halt in my driveway. A large, white settler-type man ran into my room and shouted, "Are you Dr Forbes?" He told me that I had to come to his house immediately. His new wife had just given birth and the baby was severely ill at their home. I advised him to take the baby to the hospital for proper management. He then grabbed me by the arm and ordered me to come with him right away. I had already developed a sort of fearful respect for these rough, uncouth post-colonial whites so I followed Don Coombs's orders and rode with him to his home.

There I found his beautiful wife cradling their newborn whose neck was stiffly drawn back. He was hot, screaming in a high-pitched way. I immediately recognized this as neo-natal meningitis and ordered Don to drive us immediately to the hospital. He adamantly refused shouting, "That's where he got this infection and the bastards told me he would be okay, so do what you have to do right here!" I saw the futility of any objections and asked him to drive me to my ward where I picked up the tools necessary to provide the proper treatment.

We rushed back and I instructed Don how to hold the screaming baby while I performed a lumbar puncture—one of the most difficult procedures for a newborn. The fluid came gushing out, cloudy and whitish, confirming the diagnosis of bacterial meningitis. In those days we gave "triple therapy" until the culture results in the CSF (cerebral spinal fluid) were negative. I administered the intra-muscular chloramphenicol and penicillin and oral sulpha and took the spinal fluid to the lab. The next day when I returned the baby had markedly improved. I then arranged to admit the child at the nearest private hospital, the Aga Khan, for continued treatment. The child made a then-rare complete recovery. He has grown up to be a healthy young man who is taking over his father's business with his own son now at university in Australia. Don became a good friend and continued to bully me all through East Africa. The friendship became most evident after he discovered that his grandfather was born in Jamaica of a prominent slave-owning family who now still own vast tracts of land in Montego Bay.

After a few months at Muhimbili, despite the interruptions and interference of Dr Mohammed and the nursing sister, I decided to try another approach to this type of pediatrics. I analysed the admissions to my ward and determined that the majority of those who died came from a particular village called Kisiju.

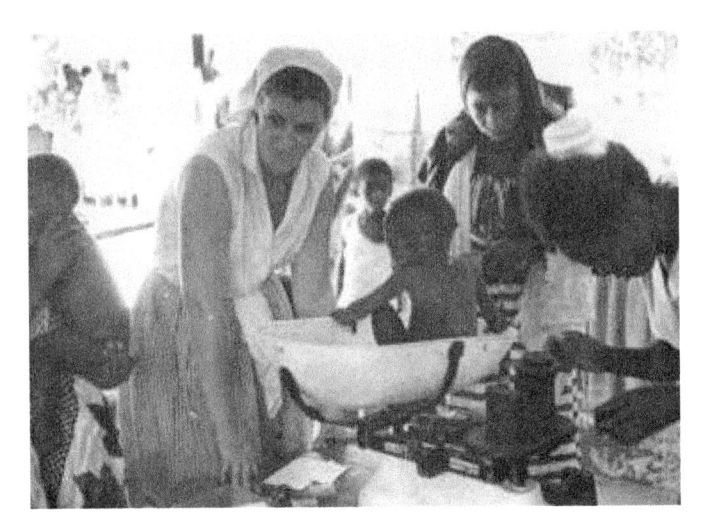

Margaret at Kisiju.

I found that this place was on the coast, about 60 miles south of Dar es Salaam. I mentioned this to a few people including a young ward assistant named Archibald Mareale, from the Chagga tribe on the slopes of Mount Kilimanjaro. Archie told me that the Kisiju people were a primitive tribe of coastal Muslims whose entire life was governed by a mixture of African voodoo beliefs (*wasi-wasi*) and Islamic customs. He warned me never to go near the village.

I discussed the situation with Margaret and she quickly saw the importance of getting to these children in their village before their diseases reached such an advanced stage that any sort of intervention was futile.

Archie, driver and patient at Kisiju.

We urged Archie to give it a try so the next week we made a reconnaissance trip to Kisiju. The 60 miles turned out to be 600 light years away from Dar. These were not all-weather roads; we passed dispersed villages, an abundance of snakes and wildlife. It took us about two and a half hours of a back-breaking Land Rover journey to reach our village. It was actually quite a beautiful place right on the Indian Ocean. The huts were mud and wattle with palm frond roofs. The beach was scattered with 13th century Chinese pottery pieces. With Archie's help we met with the village elders, the local religious leaders and the government representatives. We outlined our plan to establish a health clinic at the village which we would attend once a week and help children to deal with health problems before they grew too severe. All the folks whom we met were more than anxious to welcome us for this program.

Margaret was overjoyed and her nursing vows kicked in. Back in Dar she quickly drew up a plan for us to operate the mobile clinic weekly. She enrolled the willing help of a number of Canadian expatriate wives. We established a duty roster and we decided to pre-package our commonly used drugs such as chloroquine for malaria, penicillin, eye ointment, paracetamol for fever and packets of electrolytes to mix with coconut water for diarrhoea. Slowly the attendance at the clinic grew and we were overwhelmed. We enlisted the Canadian wives under Margaret's supervision and many local volunteer helpers, interpreters and health educationalists. I examined each child brought to me with a weight and height and immunization chart already completed. I gave each child who had obvious bacterial infection an injection of penicillin and those with strongly suspected malaria with oral chloroquine. We liberally dispensed follow-up doses.

Canadian volunteers with student.

We used to bring packed lunches and drinks and take a mid-day break to sit down under a tree and eat. We quickly realized that the surrounding villagers looked longingly at us but had no such opportunity to eat or drink. We decided that it was unfair to do this so we stopped our lunch breaks. After a heavy breakfast at home we waited until we returned to eat. That was okay by me as I have never been a lunch person but in the heat of the coastal village it was essential for me to keep up my fluids and electrolytes. The answer was fortunately close at hand and persistently provided by the village women in the form of copious amounts of coconut water. It is an ideal rehydration fluid and I gladly gurgled the water of many coconuts but as is natural, what goes in must come out. One afternoon after drinking much coconut water, I was forced to go to relieve myself. I usually did this in a nearby bush but I was proudly shown the *choo* (toilet) the village had constructed for me. It was a lovingly built wall of coconut palms with a discrete depression in the sand pointing the way, so to speak.

I was enjoying my newly found urological bliss as only a man with an overfull bladder can attest to when I suddenly heard a rustling directly in front of me. I looked straight ahead and just a-winking and a-blinking at me was an enormous python. I quickly exited my *choo* and ran through the masses of bui-bui-clad women. In my hurry, I had forgotten to replace my manhood so it was preceding me in a wobbly dangling fashion. This was immediately and inevitably noted by the throng of Muslim women to whom such exposure is anathema so they quickly raised their bui-bui masks and began loudly ululating as is the custom in such unexpected sinful circumstances. I quickly corrected that mistake and nonchalantly continued to examine my babies.

I had been soundly criticized by the other pediatrician for taking time off from my classroom teaching and taking medical students into the bush. On one of our last clinics, I realized that the child in front of me was extremely ill so we offered to take the one-year-old baby back with us to Dar to see if we could save him. His mother held him on her lap as we bumped our way back in the darkness. We then heard a deafening scream from the mother as she realized that her child had died in her arms. We stopped the vehicle and waited until she performed some strange rituals on the baby's body and then thrashed around on the ground wailing. Archie and I tried to help her. We found a local hotel where she could stay the night with her baby until she caught a bus back to her home in the morning. At the hospital I had witnessed the devastating effect of the death of a child on the mother and the seemingly mandatory ritual that ensued. The ritual seemed to help this woman to deal with this common end to children.

The incident forced me to increase my efforts even more in an attempt to alleviate this horrible suffering. By the time we had completed our two years at Kisiju we were pleased to find out that in the previous three months there had been no newborn tetanus reported, the measles rate was drastically reduced and there were no new cases of whooping cough or polio. On our last day the word must have got around to all the surrounding area also. Four hundred children attended with their parents (fathers came also!). Margaret and I, our Canadian helpers, and our students worked flat out until sundown. As we prepared to leave for the last time I could sense something important about to happen. We were joined by the chief and the imam from the local mosque. They brought the crowd to order and made speeches of thanks and praise. Then came the gift-giving ceremonies, which deeply touched us—the old lady who gave us a cooking pot and others who presented us with fly swatters, a bunch of bananas, and endless beads and bracelets that we cherish to this day. I never cease to marvel at the kindness, gratitude and generally civilized behaviour of the fine folk whom I had been taught were savages.

My two-year Canadian external aid contract was drawing to a close. I requested another African posting and fortunately I received a letter from Dr Koye Ransome Kuti from Lagos inviting us to stop over in West Africa on our way back to Canada. I had met Koye when we were SHOs (senior house officers) at Great Ormond Street. He was an imposing Nigerian doctor, the son of a prominent Anglican bishop. He had trained in Ireland and had been the resident assistant physician (RAP) in the country branch of GOS in a village called Tadworth. This was a unit initially established to care for post-operative orthopedic cases in an attempt to give the child as much fresh air as possible and freedom from the horrible germs that threatened to destroy the bone operation with osteomyelitis. Being in a long-term facility, Koye had duties that were relatively relaxed and he could come into London for our weekly grand rounds at GOS. After my presentation at one of these meetings Koye introduced himself and we quickly bonded as we were the only resident staff of obvious African descent.

Koye invited me to tea and I gladly accepted as I was by then an aficionado of the English tea—a sumptuous meal in itself bursting with sardine and cucumber sandwiches, shortbreads and cakes galore and pots of tea. All these were served to us politely and rather stiffly by English nurses in their starched uniforms. I couldn't help but wonder at the sight of all these high- class white women serving us Africans a meal, quite the opposite of what I was later to witness in Africa. Koye had an ulterior motive. He explained that Dr Bob Collis, a renowned polo-playing Irish octogenarian pediatrician who had been the professor in the Lagos University Department of Pediatrics, was about to retire so he had asked Koye to return to Lagos to take over this post. Koye was overwhelmed by the prospect and implored me to come to Lagos to join him. I discussed it with Margaret, who gave me her usual reply: "If that is what you want, Colin, then let's go."

We flew back to Montreal and the Canadian government agreed to support me in my new post in Lagos. We prepared for yet another move into a new country, by now a much-experienced task, but always daunting. Our dear friends Max and Eileen were again at hand to help us. Max had by this time quit doctoring and was desperately trying to improve his guitar and singing skills to emulate their family friend Leonard Cohen whose song "Halleluiah" was getting nationwide acclaim. Max's version sounded not the slightest bit like Leonard's. We moved into an apartment near to the Montreal Children's Hospital and Margaret was admitted to Hotel Dieu Hospital for treatment of her now moderately severe varicose veins by a vascular surgical specialist who was sourced for us by our friend and neighbour Dr Claude Joubert. I took all the children to our wonderful female pediatrician, Dr Edith James, who expertly brought my five children's immunizations up to date.

In those days we routinely offered baby aspirin post-injection so I bought a bottle and administered all their doses in our apartment. Chaos reigned as I had to prepare their meals and visit Margaret in the hospital. I happened to spot my twin boy, Carl, quietly and continuously picking up the last few aspirin he had emptied from an almost full bottle. Recognizing this as an emergency, I grabbed Carl and ran across Atwater Street to the Montreal Children's Hospital (MCH) leaving the other four children in the apartment in the care of Max and Eileen. The duty emergency doctor was my friend Hy

Goldman, who quickly took Carl and expertly performed the necessary but traumatic stomach wash out, removing a large quantity of potentially fatal aspirin tablets. Hy decided to keep Carl in the ICU overnight for observation so I returned to the chaos of my apartment. The next day I collected Margaret from hospital, both legs swathed in bandages, then picked up Carl from the ICU as docile and obedient as ever.

We left that night for Lagos, all tired, worn-out and excited. Again Carl ran his cars all over the accessible areas of his airplane seat with accompanying engine noises. After the mandatory layover in London with my sister and her now increasing family of two girls we were again Africa bound.

Chapter Fifteen

NIGERIA

Lagos was a unique experience. It was hot, bustling, disorganized and all-together daunting. It is said that once Bob Hope was visiting Nigeria on an official US government mission. On arrival in Lagos he got off the plane and was warmly greeted by the US ambassador. Bob Hope then turned up his famous nose, sniffed and asked the ambassador, "Your Excellency, what is it that I am smelling?"

The ambassador snickered and quickly replied, "It's shit!".

"Yes I know, but what did they do to it?" Bob asked. Anyone who has lived in Lagos can understand this story.

Koye drove us across town to the university enclave Surulere where we were provided a large, comfortable house. At night, however, our relative comfort was jolted by the invasion of mosquitoes that seemingly spread the word about the new Canadians in town, all the more to suck our blood. We had been assured that as our bedroom was upstairs and air conditioned we would be free from mosquitoes. Well, the diabolical little beasts did not understand that message and nightly I would go into the children's bedrooms, remove their nets and with the palms of both my hands kill the black swath of blood-filled mosquitoes outlining my children's bodies. Eventually, with a mixture of burning coils, sprays, improved nets and vigilance we were able to control the pests. I am acutely sensitive to mosquito bites so I had learned from my days in Dar that one function of the *British Medical Journal* at bedtime was to swat the beasts. Unfortunately they often landed on Margaret asleep beside me and the not-too-gentle blow of the *BMJ* on her near-naked body often woke her up with a jolt and eventually became a major problem in our otherwise deeply loving relationship.

Margaret and I decided that however impetuous and frequent our many moves were now becoming, we would not compromise on our children's education. Fortunately there exists in many countries a series of "international schools". In Africa they are mainly based on the American educational system with the staff being mainly American. We relied heavily on these schools and the education our children received from the schools' excellent dedicated American teachers was first class. In Nigeria the American school was located on Ibeji Island, a de facto expatriate enclave in steaming, bustling Lagos. Fortunately I had shipped my newly purchased Peugeot 405 station wagon from Dar so this trusty vehicle (pre-air conditioning) was used to shuttle my five children to school daily. I hired a driver as the trip was a two-hour one through the horrendous traffic of Lagos. Mile-long road blocks were common—light-heartedly called "go slows". My driver was a large, good-hearted Yoruba, with appropriate tribal facial markings, whose name was Innocent. Daily, we poured our five children into the station wagon, kissed them goodbye and implored Innocent to care for them and drive carefully. He smilingly assured us and zoomed off. He drove through the early morning Lagos traffic now at snail's pace with his hand out of the window and his fingers adeptly signifying impending lane and speed changes. Living so close to the hospital, I walked home for lunch and my well-established post-colonial routine. I would usually forgo a formal meal and speed upstairs with my glass of coconut water, undress and jump into bed under the ceiling fans. After my nap I dressed and ran downstairs to await the return of my children from school. Innocent would drive up our driveway and he, Margaret and I, together with our trusty house-help Susan, would tackle the daunting and heart-breaking task of lifting our sleeping children covered with sweat and take them to their bedrooms.

We quickly made friends with my fellow medical staff and it was not long before we were deeply involved in the vibrant social life of the hospital. It included the seemingly never-ending occurrence of weddings of my resident staff and nurses. Once it was known that Margaret and I enjoyed dancing to high-life tunes, I was often invited to be the master of ceremonies at these affairs.

Our first invitation was announced by an elaborate card that stated the event would start at 8 pm. Margaret and I duly prepared ourselves, tucked the children into bed and gave appropriate advice to Susan, who was our babysitter. We drove over to the hall where the reception was to be held. I thought I was in the wrong place as there were no other cars and the hall was in semi-darkness. I showed a passerby my invitation card to check that I was indeed at the right place. He glanced at the card, looked at me, sucked his teeth and said, "Nigerians are so awful. They got no right to put 8 pm on the card. It won't start till 10 or 11 pm. Go home, Boss, have a good rest and come back."

We followed this advice ever after. There is much formality at a Nigerian party. When the guests arrive, rarely before 11 pm, the meeting is called to order by introducing the guest who would introduce the master of ceremonies. This usually involved a lengthy curriculum vitae of the speaker plus a full recitation of his degrees and titles: Dr, the Honourable, Lieutenant General, Professor, Sir, and so forth. As master of ceremonies I was usually asked after all of the speeches to "open the dancing". Margaret and I gladly jumped up and demonstrated our now proficient high-life dance moves. We would be left alone on the dance floor while the music went on and on. By this time we would be covered with sweat and certainly running out of breath. I would implore the guests to join us and soon the dance floor would be jumping with the rest of the guests so Marg and I could escape unnoticed.

The next highlight would be the presentation of the food, some of which bore resemblance to my Jamaican food: yams, breadfruit, hot meats, and so forth. At one party I had to draw the line on being offered the opening dish, a loudly announced *piece de resistance*—snails, imported from Benin especially for the occasion. They were laid in front of us and during a loud, much-acclaimed music piece I was able to pass them on to my nearby neighbours. It was difficult for me to understand why when eating certain foods I would get an uncomfortable burning feeling in my mouth and sometimes would be violently sick. After awhile, with discrete detective work I realized that one of the most popular Nigerian dishes was ground-up shrimp. I explained my allergy so the word quickly spread and at all subsequent Nigerian feasts someone would be posted to help me to avoid the shrimp (*foofoo*).

The academic life at Lagos University Teaching Hospital—LUTH—was as vibrant as was the social one. I quickly bonded with a number of students who showed an interest in pediatrics. I had them over to our house weekly for a journal club: a review of the journals we had read that week accompanied by a lovely meal presented by Margaret and our children and washed down with good beer. Another bond I formed was with other staff and students who were tennis aficionados. We formed the LUTH tennis club and played many enjoyable games on the nearby courts with occasional tournaments. An 80-year-old American professor of medicine was the leader in this club. He took great delight in beating the pants off the young Nigerian students.

Lagos Med. School tennis club.

I was regularly visited by an eloquent Nigerian man who knew of my interest in books and introduced me to prominent Nigerian writers such as Chinua Achebe. He often visited me at night and we had an informal book club. I provided copious amounts of brandy and we listened to good music. One morning we came down to our living room to find that our home had been broken into. We lost our record player, radio, some valued mementos and all my liquor. The campus police came and quickly identified the thief as my friend and book club partner. But the incident demonstrated the incredible warmth and compassion of the Nigerian people, many of whom we barely knew, who quickly came to our house bearing gifts, flowers, food and pouring out their condolences to us in our loss.

One Sunday afternoon when I was taking my African siesta, I was awakened and told to come to the children's out-patient department. Quickly, I rushed over to find a teenage girl who had gone berserk. She was thrashing around in her bed and foaming at the mouth. I approached her quietly to see if I could calm her down when she grabbed my arm and bit into it. I quickly realized that the child had rabies and was demonstrating the classic signs of hydrophobia—foaming at the mouth and fear of water. We quickly sedated her by injection, but in those days rabies to this extent was invariably fatal. She died a couple days later despite our efforts. I was left with the very risky situation of having been bitten by a rabid patient. There was little else to do but thoroughly clean the wound and administer the rabies anti-serum injection directly into the wound. I would also receive a series of rabies vaccinations. At the time the vaccination was prepared from rabbit brains and was administered as a series of about 16 injections, 8 on either side of the abdomen! I realized that this was my only chance of preventing this deadly disease, so I dutifully received my course of abdominal injections. Unfortunately this put me out of the approaching end-of-term tennis tournaments. But fortunately I made a complete recovery after about two months.

My professional life was enriched by my eager, bright students and brilliant fellow pediatric staff. The only other expatriate in the pediatric department was Dr Ahmed, a bright, hard-working Pakistani who was devoted to helping Africa. He and his wife were overly protective of their little three-year-old daughter. One weekend we went out of Lagos together to a nearby resort island. My children were eager to play with the little girl Farah but we noticed that their approaches were gently rebuffed. I eventually asked Dr Ahmed why he did not allow Farah to play with my children. He explained that she was very light skinned, a much sought-after physical attraction in Pakistan, and overdue exposure to the African sun might tan her skin, thereby spoiling her desirability for marriage. I looked at my own children, now a deep dark colour, and wondered if I should emulate Dr Ahmed for their own future protection. I didn't and they continued to blacken beautifully.

Bad things started happening in Nigeria. A strong leader from the Eastern Region whipped up his Ibo tribe to the point where they demanded secession from the rest of Nigeria. General Ojukwu was bent on establishing the nation of Biafra. The Nigerian government, ever-changing and overwhelmed by corrupt leaders, found themselves embroiled in a full-scale civil war. As in all wars, horrible deeds were committed by both sides. Ojukwu found a powerful ally that he exploited to the hilt—the foreign press. Endless headlines screamed how the Yoruba Nigerian forces were causing untold distress to the poor people in Biafra. They even exposed the supposed atrocities committed in the LUTH pediatric wards where I worked. They said that Ibo children were developing kwashiorkor due to enforced malnutrition. I could deny such allegations but unfortunately the Canadian government got caught up in this propaganda and warned me not to be involved in such horrible behaviour. I tried in vain to refute the claims.

Lagos mother bearing gifts.

One Sunday afternoon our campus home was shaken by a feeble explosion. Looking outside we saw that a small aircraft had just pushed a home-made bomb through the door in an attempt to bomb our hospital. Fortunately it failed. Shortly afterwards we were informed by the Canadian High Commission that we were to be evacuated urgently back to Canada. Margaret and the children left shortly afterwards and I stayed behind to complete the evacuation.

Chapter Sixteen

BACK TO CANADA

In Montreal, we again tried to settle down as a family. I got the children into an upper-class private school in Montreal and set about the daunting task of delivering them there each morning before I reported to work back at the Montreal Children's Hospital. I kept in close contact with the Canadian External Aid department, now called CIDA (the Canadian International Development Agency). I was eager to return to Africa to continue my lifelong ambition of teaching and practising pediatrics there. Fortunately, at that time our new prime minister, Pierre Elliot Trudeau, was establishing himself as a deeply concerned friend of the forgotten continent of Africa. He had already made a visit to some of the newly independent nations and he developed a plan to give a gift of support for their newly established medical schools. My university, McGill, was offered the opportunity to establish the Department of Pediatrics and Medicine in the new University of Nairobi Medical School.

Formerly, East African doctors were trained at medical schools in the UK, rarely in the US or the USSR. Now Canada was offering this gift. The only medical school in East Africa at the time was Makerere in Kampala, Uganda. It was an established institution of some repute with mostly British senior staff. Professor Alan Ross, the chair of the McGill Department of Pediatrics and one of my most respected and beloved teachers, was in charge of the program at the new medical school of the University of Nairobi in Kenya. He was impressed with my previous African experience and offered me a post, which I gladly accepted.

He had already arranged with the government of Kenya to meet with two of their representatives in Montreal to discuss the details of the program. He asked me to meet these two highly placed Kenyan doctors at the railway station to bring them to our hospital. I drove out to the station in the snow to meet them. There were no African doctors there. I then called McGill to be told that two strange doctors were waiting for me at Montreal West station. They had mistaken it for Montreal Windsor station. I quickly drove to Montreal West to find two freezing African doctors impatiently pacing the platform. They were Dr Njoroge Mungai, then minister of health, and Dr Felix Onyango, then permanent secretary in the ministry. I apologized profusely for the misunderstanding and we all packed into my unheated Borgward and went to the MCH.

They were welcomed heartily with many apologies then given comfortable hotel rooms. The following day we began the formal arrangements for the program with the signing of many documents. Fairly soon the McGill team was assembled. In the meantime the war in Nigeria had ended and the Canadian government urged me to return there to complete my assignment.

LAGOS AGAIN

Our family returned to Lagos and we continued our life more or less as we left off. I was approached by Professor Bob Collis, who urged me to accompany him to northern Nigeria. A new university had been established in a town called Zaria. It was the Ahmadu Bello University, named after one of the outstanding northern Nigerian leaders. Zaria was a unique walled city, rich in history and tradition. At one of the many welcoming events we were treated to a ceremony, a *durbah,* where mounted, veiled horsemen rode at full gallop towards us in the dais with spears at the ready then suddenly reigned their horses up as we were about to be crushed to death, no doubt. This scared the shit out of me but Bob Collis, being an extremely accomplished horsemen and polo player, screamed in delight. Bob wanted me to take the newly established post of professor of pediatrics at Amadu Bello University. He introduced me to the staff and we toured the hospital, an imposing, incongruous building in this ancient Islamic setting. I was shown the living quarters that would be provided for me and my family. It consisted of a main house opening into a quadrangle lined by four smaller units. The main house was for me, they explained, the others would be occupied by my four wives and children.

On return, I explained the prospect to Margaret. She was a bit surprised but anxious to test out my newly exalted post as professor of pediatrics in one of the prestigious schools in northern Africa. In Lagos I resumed contact with McGill who assured me that the deal had been sealed. I explained my problem to Allan Ross and he assured me that he understood my dilemma but he wanted me to join the McGill Nairobi team at its onset to ensure its immediate success. He urged me to join the team even for its first year then I could return to Nigeria to take up my post. I discussed this with Bob Collis and we agreed that this would be an acceptable arrangement.

So, we were to proceed to Nairobi from Lagos for one year. Allan Ross sent an emissary from MCH, Dr Jack Charters, who would be the interim McGill team leader. The preparation to leave Lagos was an elaborate and exciting one. Many parties were thrown for us by our Nigerian friends. The most elaborate was organized by Koye Ransome Kuti himself at the popular Oasis nightclub. His brother Fela Kuti was rising to the top of the Nigerian music scene. His afro-beat music was replacing the high-life and was gaining international recognition. Fela's band was the highlight of our going away party so we danced into the wee hours of the morning. Jack Charters and his wife Stella accompanied us and were duly impressed by African hospitality and fun.

Chapter Seventeen

NAIROBI

On arrival in Nairobi we were struck by the vast difference between West and East Africa. Nairobi was cool, a mile high on the equator, very British with no national dress and with stiff, unsmiling civil servants receiving us. The highways were tidy, clean and lined with bougainvillea, jacarandas and poinsettias. From the airport we drove past the national park with giraffe, zebras, ostrich and monkeys welcoming us.

Welcome to Nairobi (Airport Road).

We spent our first days in the Fairview Hotel, a clean and comfortable family hotel still owned by a Jewish family who had been repatriated to East Africa from the European pogrom. Its owner, Claude Solomon, remains a good friend.

Our first visit was to the King George the Fifth Memorial Hospital, otherwise known as the African hospital. This colonial era medical service institution was segregated, large, basic and not clean. My pediatric ward was a converted garage with mud floors.

We met the chief of the government pediatric services. He was a smooth-talking Indian named Dr Ali Karam. He spoke the now familiar racist language of the colonials: the Africans were unable to look after themselves; they were illiterate, unkempt, unsanitary people who needed to be cared for in a strict, defined way. Any other approach was bound to fail so we must not be seen to be extra concerned by the plight of these benighted souls. I found this difficult to stomach having heard it all before in Tanzania, again from Indian doctors. The McGill team seemed to be confused by this approach from the leading government pediatrician and I found it my duty to rant and rave against this racism. I demanded that we disassociate ourselves from Dr Karam and his racist views and practices. Jack Charters was upset by my violent reaction and my demand for a de facto revolution. Quietly and smilingly, Jack sucked on his reloaded pipe saying "Well Colin, hold on! There's more than one way to skin a rabbit." Fortunately, Dr Alan Ross arrived in Nairobi with his wonderful wife and their daughter Prue. His wisdom quickly established our modus operandi and we were able to get on with the work we knew so well—teaching pediatrics. This was to be my occupation for many years, a challenging and joyous one.

Again, I found myself more interested in the socio-economic factors leading up to end-stage diseases as they presented in the hospital in their pre-morbid stages than in the fine details of the biochemical anomalies responsible for several rare diseases. Once more I took my students to rural areas to try to intervene in the ruthless ongoing march of the disease process. I taught that diseases have a straight line of progress—beginning: sore throat, cold, loose stools; middle: rheumatic fever, nephritis, dehydration; end: up to recovery, or down to the grave.

Intervening at the first stage was easy, cheap and effective. The middle stage required lab testing, some specialized drugs or IV fluids and the final stage is the "too sick too late" syndrome—the undertaker role.

So I devoted my time and efforts to concentrate on stage one of this process. This meant returning to the villages, holding under-five clinics and intervening in an appropriate way. Intervention was always done with my students who quickly learned the value of this approach. Many of these students continued their interest in "public health", as it was called, and some became leaders in various organizations such as WHO, the Christian Medical Commission and UNICEF.

Chapter Eighteen

INTERNATIONAL HEALTH

One night I was at a cocktail party in honour of a visiting Liberian bishop, Burgess Carr. I was enthusiastically expounding my views on primary health care and the necessity for mission hospitals to expand their work into the surrounding village communities. In those days Christian missions were responsible for most of the health care provided in the far-away, almost inaccessible parts of the country. Their mission stations usually consisted of a church, school, hospital and a compound that housed the missionaries, mostly white expatriates. The Protestant station would occupy one hilltop and across the village, the Catholics would be camped on another hill. My message was not to denigrate the work done by these good-hearted, well-meaning, Bible-based folk but to urge them to reach out with the same compassion to the poor people who could not afford the fees charged in their hospitals. Bishop Carr had been listening to my increasingly excited rant and he came over, drew me away from my make-believe pulpit to a chair near the bar. He explained that he agreed with everything that I said although he did not understand the deeper clinical language into which I lapsed occasionally. He explained that the World Council of Churches was holding a special session on African health at their annual meeting in Geneva the following month. He had been asked to present the African picture but he told me that he wanted me to go instead. I was more than honoured to be given such an opportunity.

I soon found myself in Geneva, surely the very opposite of the African villages that I was championing. I was overwhelmed by the hospitality, opulence and sterile cleanliness of the entire meeting venue and I was excited to meet the members of the Christian Medical Commission (CMC). This is the arm of the World Council of Churches that coordinated and supported the medical work of the member churches. The head of this commission was an Englishman named Martin McGillvary. He was an eloquent, affable but forceful proponent of primary health care. He enjoyed his whisky and we quickly bonded. He had been a missionary in Malawi. Other members of the commission were high-powered doctors such as Martin Scheel from the German Evangelical Church who had spent years in India, Dr Carl Taylor, Professor of Community Health at Johns Hopkins University, and Dick Morely from the

London University School of Tropical Medicine. Other third worlders had been invited, like me, to give firsthand reports (and colour)—Dr Gunawan Nugroho from Indonesia, the Drs Arole from India and Dr John Karefa Smart, a surgeon from Sierra Leone who became my friend when I learned that he was also a McGill graduate. He was a prominent surgeon who had been on the wrong side of a political uprising in Sierra Leone. One day he was accosted in his hospital and had his right index finger chopped off thereby putting an end to his surgical career. He was currently a professor of community health at Harvard University.

At the designated third world meeting we listened to a long and detailed paper by one of the learned American delegates who outlined his proposal to build up centres of excellence all through the third world and join them in a tenting arrangement by the newly popular computer model so we could lift up the standard of medical care all through the developing world. Africa, India, Asia and the Caribbean and Latin America would be tented up by Europe and America.

"That, my friends, is how to help the third world," he ended.

It was late, and the chairperson, Dame Nita Barrow, a Barbadian friend, wished us all good night, but I excused myself for interrupting and shouted, "With all due respect, my brothers and sisters, that is not the way to help the third world. Tenting," I explained, "is pulling from the top providing endless job opportunities for expatriate personnel. What we need is to join hands on the ground and push our efforts to help those entrapped in the morass of poverty, ignorance and disease."

By now, many in the conference room had awakened and surprisingly I got a standing and even shouting applause from all the third worlders and others eager to join our cause.

The following day I was approached by the leaders of the Christian Medical Commission to join their group. I warned them that last night was merely a taste of my "shit-disturbing" mentality and I was worried about the possible effect it would have on the group. "That is just what we need," Martin Scheel said.

Joining the CMC began a new career for me in international health. As a commissioner, I was pleased to attend many meetings in various parts of the world to continue the primary health care message. I did this in Korea, India, many parts of Africa, the Caribbean and Central America. There were also spin-offs. One day I received a telegram from the United States saying that the Vietnam War was coming to a successful close and the American Medical Association had been requested to prepare the Vietnam medical schools to switch over from the French-based curriculum to a USA one. They admitted that their team needed someone with third world experience to assist them to do this. The long telegram ended with "security guaranteed". I rushed to show this to Margaret and seek her approval. As usual, she said "If you want to go fine, but do be careful". I assured her that this was dealt with in the final two words of the telegram.

So, off I went from Nairobi to Pakistan, Thailand, then Vietnam. Strapped onto bags of rice in a US Air Force cargo plane, we landed in Saigon. I faced tired, hung-over soldiers returning to duty after a brief R&R in Thailand. I was driven in a jeep to my hotel, a down-trodden building built from American spare parts and owned by a black American sergeant who told me he had won it in a poker game. I was exhausted from the long trip and gladly flopped into my bed. I woke up in the darkness to the horrific noise of bombs exploding. I quickly got up, dressed, pushed the service button and prepared to escape.

A sleepy-eyed Vietnamese lady answered my call and asked me, "What you want?"

I said "Don't you hear the noise boom boom boom? We are under attack!"

She smiled and said "Every night boom boom boom, go back to sleep!" That was the beginning of the Tet offensive, which would lead to the defeat and ignominious departure of the US troops.

I was sent to a small town called Danang, south of Saigon, to report on the health services there. Our driver, a Vietnamese in an army jeep, pointed out the many attacks that had taken place on this road. I asked him, "How do you know who is Viet Kong?"

He turned, looked at me with the inscrutable Asian smile and said, "You never know, do one?" I cringed.

In Danang, I was put up in a seedy building that was supposed to be the local hotel but turned out to be a brothel. The lady showed me to my room, set the mosquito net and asked, "Anything you want?"

"No thanks," I replied.

"You want Vietnamese girl?"

"Not tonight," I replied

"You want boy?"

"No thanks," I insisted.

There were no mosquitoes but later that night I was surrounded by an invasion of cockroaches. I did all I could to repel them. Eventually, in despair, I took out my trusted ever-present bottle of Jamaican rum, sprinkled it generously over my bed, drank the remainder then went to sleep.

It was in Danang while sitting at breakfast in a local restaurant that I saw the world's most effective biodiversity program. My table was close to a shallow canal in which many good-sized fish frolicked. The fish were displayed on a menu printed all around the restaurant. You just pointed. I saw an elderly man climb onto what appeared to be a chair suspended over the canal. He let his trousers down and shat right into the canal. The fish (my menu) excitedly gobbled up this delicacy. *Chaque-a-sans-gout*, I thought.

We met for a presentation of our findings at the end of our assignment. One of my American colleagues, from a university in the South, arranged the presentation. He explained that we would do this in the form of role playing with each of us acting out the various roles he outlined for us. Mine was a village doctor explaining the value of hand-washing and proper food storage, preparation and cooking in preventing diarrhoeal disease. I suffer from severe irritable bowel syndrome. In the middle of my role playing I experienced the familiar cramping of impending intractable diarrhoea. I tried to warn my leader but I found it best to make discretion the better part of valour so I dashed off to the toilet just in time. I can truly say that I shat myself through Vietnam.

We met with high-ranking officials of the Vietnamese government, each group trying to outdo the other in their hospitality. One night we were at an elaborate dinner in the army headquarters. I had informed my host and minder that I was acutely sensitive to shrimp. He assured me that this information had already been conveyed to them by the US government and it was his duty to protect me so I happily and recklessly dug into my food. Soon I began to experience the tell-tale signs of my food sensitivity—burning in the mouth, sweating, abdominal discomfort and nausea. After many deep breaths I realized that I was losing the battle, so I got up and dashed to the bathroom, all this in the middle of ever-present Viet Kong terrorism. I barely made it to the toilet but fell on the floor vomiting. I looked up into the cocked rifles of some serious-looking Vietnamese soldiers. Fortunately my minder rushed in and told them not to shoot. I later learned that all Vietnamese food is doused in a sauce made of ground-up shrimp.

Back in Nairobi, I quickly became embroiled in a new health program—a cholera outbreak in western Kenya. There had been outbreaks in surrounding countries so this came as no surprise. As professor of community health I had arranged a retreat for my department in the cool hills of Limuru. We were led by a professional American facilitator, Dr Abigail Krystal. Her job was to improve the educational performances of the various departments of the medical school. She did this skillfully through a variety of methods including group workshops, role playing and some old-time lectures. My department benefitted greatly from this retreat. At the end we decided that one of our tasks was to involve the entire department, including the students, in structuring the curriculum each term. It was no wonder that on our return to Nairobi the department decided that we would teach all aspects of community health by active involvement in the cholera control program in western Kenya.

We divided the entire department into various committees, each having autonomous control of their activity: transport, food, housing, safety, statistics, and cooperation with existing programs including the government supervised one. The Russians provided experienced physicians; the Japanese established laboratories. I visited the area and explained our impending involvement. We then assembled for our long trip to Kisumu. On our arrival we were shown the facilities chosen as our lodgings. The student leaders took one look and completely refused to consider them as being suitable. I had no choice but to arrange accommodation in a nearby mission station—far cleaner and more comfortable. The following day we decided to split up into groups and visit various villages most affected by the epidemic. I remember driving out of the town to see a long line of struggling villagers trying to reach the nearby cholera station. A few did not make it and dropped dead on the road. I realized that cholera should be called "epidemic diarrhoea in poor people" because death was mostly from the severe dehydration that quickly attacked the sufferers. Rapid intervention with enormous amounts of IV fluids and electrolytes almost always was life saving but this could only be done in a well-established centre to which the poor had limited access.

A member of my department, an American named Roy Schaffer, devised a unique way of keeping track of our teams and keeping in contact during our widespread village programs. He distributed helium balloons to the various cholera stations. While doing this, a cry suddenly went up from one of our energetic and vocal department members, a large Dutch doctor named John Mahue. "De balloons," he shouted. We witnessed all of the balloons released from their secure post in the Land Rover floating serenely over the plains.

Our efforts bore fruit as we defined a particular village that had virtually no cases of cholera. We learned that this village was the stronghold of a religious group called Legio Maria, a break-away sect of the Roman Catholic church led by a defrocked priest. They had strict Old Testament hygiene rules—vigorous hand washing, no hand shaking, proper waste disposal, no pork, all food cooked thoroughly, drinking water boiled and many other rigid Old Testament food laws. We asked the leaders of this group to accompany us to advise the surrounding villages in adapting these control measures. The program was a great success and soon we were able to pronounce our designated area cholera free.

We returned triumphantly, having demonstrated in a practical way that the University Medical School teaching in the context of existing health problems was of great value. Buoyed by this acknowledged success I was eager to continue extending our department activities to the areas of Kenya that had a great need of more health care.

I realized that the northern areas, towards the Ethiopia and Somali borders, were devoid of health-care facilities except for a few isolated mission hospitals.

These services were supported by an energetic old Swiss doctor, Dr Ann Spoerry, who flew a fancy aircraft donated by various governments through the African Medical Research and Educational Foundation (AMREF)—the Flying Doctors. The foundation had been established by an ex-colonial plastic surgeon, Dr Michael Wood, himself a pilot who flew into isolated medical posts, providing much needed health support. Mike was an amazing man and I quickly bonded with him, flying to many far-away posts in Kenya and Tanzania. There we would spend two days with Mike operating on a great number of needy patients and me providing health-care intervention and advice to the many children who were gathered there.

Dr Spoerry was formerly a member of AMREF but her independence and obstinacy inevitably clashed with Wood's AMREF empire. I joined Ann on many of her trips to northern Kenya outposts. One morning, on preparing to leave a mission after spending an exhausting day, I saw Ann, then in her seventies, crawling along the wing of her aircraft filling the gas tanks. I offered to help but she refused. I asked her to consider asking the African assistant who was designated to help her. She rudely barked "Let one of those fill my petrol tank? No way! That's how my friend died when his tank was filled with water!"

On a flight from northern Kenya to Nairobi I noticed that Ann had put the plane on auto-pilot and then went to sleep. It was a long trip over a mostly deserted area so I was OK with that, but as we neared Nairobi, the Aberdare Mountains appeared and I calculated that our present altitude would not be sufficient to clear them. I pondered over my next move but decided to brave it and wake Ann up.

She awoke and asked "What's the matter?"

"The Aberdares," I replied.

"We got a couple of hundred feet to clear them." Then she promptly went back to sleep.

Ann Spoerry also did much needed work at the Kenya coast. I joined her on one of her many trips to the small island of Lamu. These virtually self-sufficient outposts were inhabited by Swahili people who rarely connected to the mainland. They also had no access to mainland health care so Ann was their only link to modern medicine. Ann had a house on Lamu, one of the beautiful centuries-old Arab structures which she had lovingly converted into a comfortable home. We landed on the mainland airstrip serving both Lamu and Shela on the island and went by boat to Shela where her house was. We were met by a host of excited Swahili people who drove us there. Being a classic Arab-Swahili home, there was a courtyard where visitors sat waiting to be invited in. The courtyard was packed with sick people waiting for "Daktari" to heal them. She immediately went to work at this sick parade and I offered to help her. She sent me all the children and I tried my best.

When we were finished, our host, Juma, who was in complete charge of the home, settled us with a warm bath and a generous supply of gin and tonics. The meal was amazingly delightful and Juma and his wives cared for us with kindness and love. Ann Spoerry's funeral at the All Saints Cathedral in Nairobi was well attended with representatives from the AMREF dynasty, Kenyan, Swiss and Tanzanian governments and a strong Arab-Swahili contingent from the coast. I was able to squeeze into a seat at the back of the cathedral.

At the Department of Community Health we had successfully obtained a large area of Machakos District for rural health teaching programs. We defined three villages, Mwala, Masi and Mitaboni, as the focal points of our department teams, each under the control of a group of lecturers. We were most fortunate to gain the cooperation and trust of the leaders of these communities and with persistent effort we were able to have a measurably positive effect on their health. Machakos is the home of the Kamba tribes people. They had the reputation of being fierce warriors and indeed they were said to have had fierce battles with the neighbouring Kikuyu over the establishment of Nairobi. During the Second World War a battalion of African soldiers, the King's African Rifles, rendered fine service to the British Empire forces. Many of these soldiers were Kamba. The KAR fought valiantly in Burma. All their officers were, of course, white Kenyan settlers. They were devoted to their "fine boys" and supported them well. At the end of the war the white officers were richly rewarded with land and prominent posts within the colonial government while the African soldiers received a pittance and "thank you" on their return.

This unfair treatment created an undertow of dissatisfaction and was in part the nidus of a rebellious movement called the Mau Mau, led by Kikuyu tribesmen whose leader was Jomo Kenyatta. Thirty-eight whites were killed and many thousands of Africans lost their lives. The British government, headed by Prime Minister Sir Alfred McMillan, warned the world of the "changing wind which was blowing across Africa"—a wind that would rapidly see the end of the British Empire. French, German, Spanish and eventually Portuguese colonies were also dismantled and handed over to the "natives" for self-rule. Freedom created immediate exuberance and exhilaration, but the stiff hand of local leaders quickly grabbed the finances, land and positions of power. This often meant settlement of old tribal disputes, some of which led to civil wars, always hindering the progress of the new nations. Many of the leaders were overthrown. Example: Kwame Nkrumah in Ghana, many Nigerian presidents, Obote of Uganda, to be followed by his conqueror Idi Amin. The outstanding leader of the newly independent African nations was Julius Nyerere, a humble, Edinburgh educated teacher who ruled Tanzania with integrity, intelligence and benevolence. Unfortunately, his socialist regime of Ujamaa was interpreted by the West as being communist so they quickly brought it to its knees.

Nyerere was one of the few African independence leaders who resigned his post. I had the honour of meeting this remarkable man on many occasions and his wisdom and humility were most impressive. The Kenya scene was quite different. The country was taken over mostly by the Kikuyu tribesmen of Jomo Kenyatta. They claimed this position by virtue of their predominance in the independence struggle. A leader of a rival tribe, a Luo, from the western area bordering on Lake Victoria, was an intellectual named Oginga Odinga. He had studied in Russia and was deemed by the West to be communist. He was the first vice president for awhile but was soon deposed and sent out to Luo-land to pasture. His son, Raila Odinga, was vice president of Kenya after a bitter election struggle. Please don't talk to me about democracy. In the African context, one man one vote means "Who will give that man the most money, or food, or futile promises of a job if he will vote for *me*?" When will the West learn that and devise some other method of true representation?

Chapter Nineteen

PRIVATE PRACTICE

Independence also carried with it not so pleasant aspects of social life. For us on the McGill team, it was manifested as a kind of reverse racism. The chief government pediatrician was a Pakistani who quickly informed us of the inappropriateness of our Western pediatrics. He emphasized the futility of trying to save the lives of African children. "They have too many children anyhow, allow them to die in peace." That meant struggling for breath from choking in measles LTB (laryngo-tracheo-bronchitis) or coughing themselves to death from whooping cough, or dying a painful death from lock jaw (tetanus), or starving to death from kwashiorkor, and so forth. In my efforts in primary care programs I was often mocked by the cognoscenti, including African doctors, explaining the futility of trying to get the poor, ignorant villagers to serve as members of their own health team. Nevertheless, we continued in our efforts to teach proper "McGill pediatrics" in the African setting. One of our jobs was to identify Kenyan post-graduate students who would eventually return as the leaders of the Department of Pediatrics. A few of these doctors rose to the top as possible candidates and we convinced McGill to fund their training at the Montreal Children's Hospital. Nimrod Bwibo was one of the first of these, followed by Julius Meme and a host of others. They all returned to high posts in the Ministry of Health. Nimrod became the vice chancellor of the university. After five years, the McGill contract ended and all Canadians returned to Montreal except for me.

In 1977 I left the McGill team and sought other gainful employment. I asked CIDA to employ me in other areas of child health in Africa—no luck. I heard of great opportunities in pediatrics in Saudi Arabia so I applied. The outstanding attraction of this post was its financial reward. I could make twice as much as my McGill pay, tax free, and have endless educational opportunities for my children in the many American institutions there at that time. I went to London to be interviewed by one of these recruiting agencies. I eventually found the place on a small street off Piccadilly Circus. A sleepy hung-over Englishman looked over my papers, defined me as suitable then explained the conditions:

an enormous salary tax free, paid wherever I wanted

schooling for my children in an American school in Saudi Arabia or in a nearby country two weeks holiday in my home country (Canada) every four months for my entire family

my wife would be virtually house bound, not allowed to drive and must be accompanied on all trips outside the home by me

my wife would wear appropriate dress (the hijab)

no alcohol would be allowed

I flew home with the good news for Margaret who was waiting in Montreal with the children for the decision about our next move. I described the good news about the Saudi job, its amazing salary and frequent home leaves, which were very appealing but she was not happy about her restrictions. Anyhow, as always, she agreed to accompany me "if that is what you want to do". I had been doing a limited private practice from a specially defined room in my house but I did not have many patients. My sister Fay was living with us at the time, while spending most of the time with her Guyanese friend Don at his home in Chemelil, the heart of sugar country in western Kenya. Fay had an East Indian Guyanese friend, Rama, who was a lawyer but was now merely keeping house for her English husband Fred and their two small boys. Rama and Fred usually stayed with us in Nairobi. I told her of my dilemma in choosing our next post. She assured me that Margaret would not survive the restrictive environment of Saudi Arabia. She encouraged me to look into starting a private practice in Nairobi. I had never done this sort of medical work so she set up the entire business plan necessary. I thanked Rama for her help and advice and reminded her that by this time I was almost completely broke, facing a month's rent which I could barely afford.

I played tennis in the mornings and in the afternoons also as I waited for patients. About this time, I met a young Indian doctor, Mahendra Patel, who had a modest, store-front general practice in a marginal part of Nairobi. He offered me an examining room in his office and asked me to see any children who came. I readily did this and enjoyed being in my pediatric mode with African children who very much needed my help. One night after clinic hours I sat with Mahendra and explained my plan to re-settle in Saudi Arabia. He implored me not to go, assuring me that after awhile I could build up a satisfactory practice in Nairobi. I told him that I would discuss the idea with Margaret. The following night he told me that he had discussed the matter with his uncle, a wealthy lawyer, who offered me a substantial loan of $20,000 US to entice me to remain where I was. I could not refuse this offer as my next month's rent was imminent and school fees were due. I then seriously committed myself to private practice, first from my home, then in a building that was literally part of the large up-scale Nairobi Hospital. In that way I could gain from the many children who attended the hospital's outpatient department.

Margaret again came to my professional rescue and established the entire medical aspect of the clinic. She fortunately gained the help of a Trinidadian nurse who was able to relieve her from some of the nursing, reception and general office duties. Quickly my office became popular with the expatriate community and rich Indian and African families. Being affluent, their health problems were mostly minimal (colds, coughs, scrapes and bruises) but we had to be on guard for the ever-present serious life-threatening diseases such as malaria, meningitis, aspirin and other poisonings, tick fever and Kawasaki disease. In four months I was able to pay off my loan to Mr Patel. Fortunately I was also able to serve poor African children with whom I had been deeply involved for so many years. Some of my Maasai families followed me to my new clinic. Their lifestyle and diet (blood and cow's milk) contributed to their characteristic odour, which was not always appreciated by my fancy patients who rapidly exited the room when a Maasai family entered my clinic, sometimes after a day's walk with their sick child or adult.

CLINICAL CHALLENGES

A particularly puzzling Maasai child, Challe, had strange growths in her bones and abnormal pigmentation of her skin. I was challenged by her condition as it reminded me of a child with similar symptoms and findings I had seen a few years before in Kenyatta Hospital. After much searching I found that this disease was a rare disease with a genetic predisposition. I had managed the previous patient with a combination of drugs but unfortunately after awhile she had succumbed. I decided to use steroids in Challe in a high dose. It worked marvels. All her symptoms virtually disappeared and her parents were extremely pleased. On each follow-up visit I was unceremoniously presented with (that is, they were thrown at me) beautiful gifts—two beaded stethoscopes and many necklaces. These folks encouraged me to visit their home which I did years later. They welcomed me with much drumming, horn blowing, spear throwing and dancing by bare-chested ladies. These patients provided me with the personal and professional stimulation which in part justified my lucrative practice amongst the well-heeled and well to do.

Greeting foreign patients.

A friend of mine, Mo Eckstein, was a well-known promoter of the arts. He came to my office with an American who explained that Hollywood was producing a film called *Out of Africa*, starring Robert Redford and Meryl Streep. Meryl would bring her two children for the three months it would take to shoot the African section. She and her family would reside in Langata, a Nairobi suburb. She needed assurance that adequate pediatric assistance would be provided as necessary. For Mo to assure them that I was more than adequate, he brought a Hollywood official to inspect my office and me. We passed! So a few months later, Meryl Streep and her two children arrived at my clinic. They had just landed from Europe and she was concerned that her little son seemed to be sick in the last leg of their long flight.

She came to my registration window, and my trusted African receptionist Margaret got a card out and asked, "What's your name?"

"Meryl Streep," she replied.

"Occupation?"

Meryl smiled and replied "Actress". A strange welcome to a strange continent.

Meryl stepped into my office with her children, stopped, looked around and said, "It's so beautiful. I wish my pediatrician's office in New York was like this."

In fact, my office was a mess, with walls plastered with coloured paintings and drawings done by my patients, placed by them wherever they wanted. I humbly introduced myself and cared for her children for the rest of their stay.

On another occasion, I was greeted by an African gentleman who explained his son's symptoms and asked me for help. On completion of my examination I was making my notes when I noticed that his home address was listed as Hawaii.

"How did you, a Luo, end up in Hawaii?"

He smiled and explained that he taught in the university there. "It's a nice place," he explained.

I jokingly asked him to get me a job there. Two days later, I saw his child again, this time brought by his mother. She was a stern white American lady who immediately asked me if my fees were going to be as exorbitant as those of other doctors in Nairobi. I assured her that they would be reasonable and after re-examination of her child, I told her that he was improving satisfactorily. I later witnessed this child assuming a very high position in the US government. Nuff said.

Princes, offspring of highly placed Muslim religious leaders, many of the world's richest and Africa's most powerful families came through our doors. I was determined to offer the highest quality of pediatric care. I continuously studied my journals—*Pediatrics, Pediatric Notes, Nelson's* and its tropical counterpart, *Manson Barr*. Doing so cut deeply into my free time and inevitably, my family suffered. We managed somehow to squeeze out family time on safaris. The incredible beauty of an early morning game drive with the omniscient tour driver pointing out differences between Grant's and Thomson's gazelles, impala, kudus, oryx, and so forth followed by a campfire breakfast served by efficient and caring African staff—those safaris were a pleasure I will never forget.

I continued to teach at the university. By this time I had enough experience in pediatrics in Africa to develop my own views on managing the many so-called tropical diseases. Example: one of our scourges was African tick fever. This serious disease is related to Lyme disease and is carried by a tick with a similar organism, *Borrelia burgdorferi*. The child presents with a fever, headache and muscle pains, and stiffness leading sometimes to partial lower-limb paralysis. The giveaway sign is a scab where the tick bit and enlargement of the nearby gland; a rash may also occur. One year, many of the world's astronomers descended on Kenya to witness a rare total eclipse of the sun. They camped in a field in Machakos District and stayed up all day and night gazing at this spectacle. Weeks later, a number of these watchers succumbed to tick fever and unfortunately some of them, in their home countries, were misdiagnosed and suffered serious consequences. I know that administering tetracycline in adequate doses will cure this disease quickly so this is what I prescribed for my children.

"No, no!" came the cry from pharmacists and fellow doctors, "you cannot use tetracycline in children, it will stain their teeth."

"To hell with teeth staining," I often shouted, "I'm trying to save this child's life, and brain!"

Strange how otherwise intelligent doctors will slavishly follow an edict that has life-threatening consequences.

FRIENDS

I soon touched base with a young American cardiologist, Dan Silver, in Kenyatta Hospital and we became good friends. He was a brilliant clinician and he cared for his patients with with skill and kindness. This was not a common trait among the post-colonial expatriate doctors. Once when discussing a particularly puzzling case with some doctors in the coffee room I was told "Oh Colin, why get so worked up? This world is over-populated as it is and these Africans live such a miserable life that it would be a relief to them to be taken out of their misery."

Dan was a devout Jew and often stepped in as a rabbi at the synagogue in Nairobi. He was also a fun-loving, adventure-seeking young man who had served with the

American military in southeast Asia during the Vietnam war. He was an established bachelor whose weakness was beautiful African women or any other beauty who crossed his path. He lived in one of the staff houses near Kenyatta Hospital, so he often invited me to his house for lunch. I had already developed the African habit of a mid-day siesta and it was more valuable to me than lunch so I would greet Dan and head straight for the guest bedroom. More than once, I accidentally bumped into a beautiful lady leaving Dan's bedroom with a sheepish smile on her face.

I also met a young African doctor, James Mbaka, who had returned from many years of medical school and post-graduate training in pediatric surgery with his wife Betty, a German pediatrician, and their two daughters. James was a godsend to me as his diagnostic and operative skills were superb. His special interest was in pediatric urology and he treated many of my cases of vesicoureteral —bladder to ureter—reflux in children with resounding success. There is also a very serious congenital anomaly where the trachea (breathing tube) ends in a blind pouch often connected to the oesophagus. This is called a trachea-oesophagial fistula. It must be diagnosed early or the baby's feed ends up in the lungs and chokes the child to death. The repair of this abnormality requires the greatest surgical and anaesthetic skill and, even in large first world centres, the mortality rate is high. James worked with a skilled pediatric anesthetist named Ezekiel Bani. Zeke was a small Nigerian whose skill in handling even premature babies was impressive. We often joked that Zeke could climb up into the child's throat and skillfully insert the tube through the small opening of the vocal cords so that he could establish an airway for the anaesthetic gases and oxygen. It was a joy to work with James. When I diagnosed a particular surgical problem, such as a suspected appendicitis, I would rest assured that James would do the right thing when I referred the child to him. In those days 60% of the appendices removed at Kenyatta Hospital had already ruptured, the too-late diagnosis.

James and Betty bought an imposing house near Kenyatta Hospital and they constructed a comfortable room with an oven, benches and a nearby shower. This sauna was to become the headquarters for James and Betty, Marg and me, Dan and consort, Wasserman (an Israeli engineer) and Esther, his wife, every Wednesday night for the next 28 years. In this sauna we discussed difficult medical cases, the state of the world, local politics and raw gossip. Dan also provided us with many jokes during the cold-shower breaks. Discrete nudity was the order of the night except for undue arousal episodes which were quickly masked. After the sauna, Betty served an always wonderful meal washed down with a few German wines and Jamaican rum.

Some of the Sauna gang.

These precious weekly moments were extremely beneficial to all of us. They served as a valuable catharsis for all of our ever-present troubles, worries and fears. Once we missed Dan only to learn the next day that he was a vital organizer of the medical teams from Israel who refueled in Nairobi en route to rescue the many Israeli hostages held in Entebbe, Uganda, by the mad ruler Idi Amin. The only Israeli killed in that operation was the twin brother of the present prime minster of Israel, Benjamin Netanyahu. I was, and still am, concerned about the Palestinian people but learned quickly not to push my point as my Jewish friends were adamantly opposed to their behaviour.

Dan took flying lessons and quickly gained his pilot licence. His flying instructor assured me that Don could fly—"sort of". Dan was anxious to have me accompany him on his many excursions. Once we were granted an all-paid weekend in one of Kenya's most luxurious and costly safari camps, Little Governors in the Maasai Mara Reserve, a small camp on a river. On landing at a nearby airstrip (in reality, a dirt path) we were taken to a small boat (a sort of Venetian gondola) hand-powered by an African boatman with a long pole who sang Italian opera arias—a fascinating experience. The camp itself was a series of luxurious tents that could rival any five star hotel. The beds were elevated on wooden planks with comfortable mosquito nets and fans that worked when the generator was on. The showers were al fresco with a trusty servant pulling a rope to tip the bucket of warm water on our soapy bodies. After an afternoon rest Dan and I walked over to the dining tent for supper, which was a sumptuous affair starting with a gin and tonic sundowner as we sat under the shooting stars and full moon. The meal was magnificent with each of the five courses washed down with an appropriate wine.

When finished, I lit the offered cigar and we were just leaving when a distraught woman, obviously French, rushed over to our table and asked "You are docteurs?"

"Oui," I answered.

"Come here," she shouted as she dragged Dan over to her table, opened a bottle of pills, threw them down on the table and demanded, "Ow much of zeezees I must take to die?"

We sat her down. Dan collected the pills, returned them to the bottle and put them in his pocket.

"What's the matter," he asked, kindly holding her hand. This led to a one hour explanation of her coming to Kenya to meet her boyfriend, a bush pilot, who had flown her to this camp but then returned to Nairobi to his new girlfriend.

"He doomped me," she kept repeating.

We walked her to her tent, Dan gave her a sedative and we bade her goodnight. We asked the night watchmen to keep an eye on her and notify us if necessary. Dan kept repeating "he doomped me" until we went to sleep.

When flying back to Nairobi, Dan took his landmarks from the Ngong Hills, which resembled the four bumps of the knuckles on a closed fist. Flying between the second and third knuckle lined us up with the appropriate landing strip at Wilson Airport, then one of the busiest airports for small aircraft in Africa. My duty was to line Dan up through the knuckles so we did not run into the adjacent hills—scary sometimes.

Both Dan and James purchased land and built beautiful homes on their farms. Dan had been appointed as the personal physician of President Moi, who took over when Jomo Kenyatta died while on holiday dancing with school children at the coast. Moi had been a behind-the-scenes vice president, put there by the Kikuyu to preserve their grip over the country. He was from a small nomad tribe of the north—the Kalenjins. Thought to be a convenient pawn in the Kikuyus' hand, he actually took the opposite approach and wielded his constitutional presidential powers with an iron fist. In the last days of Jomo Kenyatta the country was virtually ruled by a small Kikuyu clique led by the attorney general, Charles Njonjo. Moi set about dismantling and emasculating this group. He eventually brought Njonjo up in court, charging him with being a traitor because of his obvious anglophile connection. He dressed like an English gentleman and indeed married a white lady of English heritage. Moi had Njonjo before the court for 144 days, parading witnesses who lied about him. Eventually, to demonstrate his largesse, Moi pardoned Njonjo, to everyone's relief.

Meeting President Moi.

During this time I continued to provide pediatric care to Njonjo's three young children. They were all under virtual house arrest so I had to visit their home in Muthaiga, an affluent part of Nairobi. Armed guards would search my car at the gate and grudgingly let me in with a warning on how to behave. I became close to the Njonjo family during this period as did James and Dan, who also cared for them. Dan, renowned for his loyal, skilled, professional care to Moi in Kenya and on the many overseas trips with him, received a 125-acre farm in Naivasha, prime agricultural land, not far from Nairobi. With one of Nairobi's foremost architects Dan quickly constructed a dream home which included a comfortable guest suite downstairs that was to become our weekend home on many occasions. Sipping sundowners on Dan's veranda, we witnessed a kaleidoscope of nature's wonders—many types of gazelles, giraffes, some rhinos and every type of African bird life. Sundowners were always followed by a sumptuous kosher meal with the finest wines. In those days, in respect to our brothers and sisters, fighting for their still-to-be-gained independence, the wine list excluded the fine South African wines and the lovely Portuguese Mateus. Fortunately Mandela's release and the Portuguese relinquishing of Mozambique and Angola freed us to partake of these fine wines.

African liberator.

James decided to build his country home in the ancestral lands of his Kamba people—the as. These hills were a high escarpment not far from Nairobi with an imposing view of the plains below and the city in the distance. James and Betty built an imposing structure on a hilltop. The agreement was that they would present the Saturday night sumptuous meal before we all sat outside to watch the aircraft from Europe coming in to land at Jomo Kenyatta Airport and the shooting stars. James also built a sauna which we approached through a path of rosemary bushes which also served to shade us in our al fresco shower. Sunday morning was my time to cook my now famous omelets which I presented with much fanfare eliciting many "cries of delight". We then sat outside for our coffee and listened to the famous BBC commentator Alistair Cooke, who invariably led us to an in-depth examination of world affairs until our mid-day rest, tea and return down the Mua Hills to Nairobi.

Our own family life was going through difficult times. Our children were all in the International School of Kenya, later to become the Nairobi International School. The American-led education system prevailed although the Canadians were later to gain partial ownership of the school. This allowed our children to attempt to fit into the Canadian educational system in anticipation of our return home. My children quickly developed a group of friends with whom they would spend most of their free time. Much of it was in our home and I often wondered what they were spending their long afternoons and evenings doing.

One afternoon I found out. I was walking outside the upstairs bedroom of one of my children and beneath the windows I saw a disgusting assortment of drug paraphernalia. There were butt ends of marijuana joints, some needles and syringes, and empty vials of a variety of psychotropic drugs. I showed the array to Margaret and we agreed that this explained the strange behaviour of our children and their friends. We approached the school about it and they assured us that this was merely a stage that many international children were going through and they would grow out of it. I took the hard line and banned all such activity in my home—to no avail, as they merely continued it elsewhere. The popular weekend night spot for those teenagers was a seedy location called the Golf Range. It was indeed an unused golf range converted into a disco. Teenagers and their hangers-on converged on this spot on the outskirts of Nairobi every weekend and freely participated in an orgy of alcohol and drugs. Inevitably there was confrontation between the various racial groups—the expatriate whites, the white settlers (Kenya cowboys), the Indians and the upper-class Africans. This often resulted in various degrees of injuries requiring evacuation to Nairobi Hospital. On two occasions intoxicated teen-age drivers were killed in crashes on leaving the Golf Range. All our older three children were deeply involved in this devastating gang activity. They have all suffered from the long-lasting effects of this behaviour and that has had a serious effect on many of our relationships.

I continued to practise my pediatrics in the best way possible and to teach in the university. My work in international health increased. I was often requested to act as an external examiner in pediatrics for final-year and post-graduate students in various universities in Africa. I did this in the nearby university of Dar es Salaam and in Makerere University in Uganda. I was once requested to be the external examiner in the Centre Universite de Sante de Cameroon (CUSC). I gladly agreed and on landing in Yaoundé I was met by a member of staff who drove me to the only habitable hotel in the city. He showed me to my room and presented me with an armful of examination books for me to correct and on which to bestow a final mark. They were all in French and thus tested my Quebec French to its hilt. I eventually got through all of them. They seemed remarkably alike to me so I wondered if there could have been collusion in the exam. I suggested this and was assured *ces't n'es pas possible*. The next morning I went to the dining room for breakfast and a waiter in a uniform that had seen much better days proudly presented me with the menu. It consisted of coffee, *pain brule* and *jus d'orange*. I anxiously awaited my meal which turned out to be half a glass of orange juice, fried bread and some tired coffee. After the examination meeting in which I presented my decisions I was assured that a cheque would be mailed to me. I was showered with many *merci beaucoup*s and sent on my way to the Yaoundé airport.

I went to the departure lounge to catch the only plane leaving for East Africa that week. I was caught in a melee of shouting, screaming folk each waving their tickets, like mine. I reached the counter, presented my first class ticket and was told the flight was all booked. I shouted that this was a confirmed first class ticket and I was a doctor on my way to Nairobi for a medical emergency. The tired lady took pity on me, adjusted her towering head gear, winked at me and tossed her head in the direction that I quickly followed. Scratching and clawing, shoving and screaming I eventually climbed aboard the creaky aircraft and got back to Nairobi.

The CMC told me of the meeting they were having in Bali, Indonesia, and asked me to attend as part of the African delegation. I gladly accepted and suggested to

Margaret that as this was our 25th wedding anniversary she accompany me to beautiful Bali then I would return to Nairobi. As an anniversary gift, she would continue on a trip around the world—to Japan and California to visit her family, then Montreal, London UK and back home to Nairobi. We arranged for the care of our children and prepared to go on our epic journey. I was told that we needed visas to go to Indonesia so I went to their embassy in Nairobi. I felt very fortunate because the Indonesian ambassador regularly attended my clinic with his children, who were suffering from a variety of illnesses, all of which I treated successfully. I explained my Bali visit and requested that the ambassador provide me with a visa. He said that this was usually a time-consuming and costly process but I could circumvent it by presenting myself at the Indonesian embassy in Singapore, which was our stop-over point to Jakarta. He explained that he had recently been posted in Singapore and he knew everyone there so I would merely present myself to the embassy bearing his card and the visas would be quickly granted. He assured me that this was foolproof and certain.

Margaret and I flew into Singapore, booked in at Raffles Hotel and enjoyed the superb oriental hospitality. The following morning I woke up early and went to the Indonesian embassy. I was surprised to find myself at the end of a long line. I explained my request and the rough security guard told me to get back into line. Eventually I reached the desk where a smiling embassy official asked me what I wanted. I proudly presented His Excellency the Indonesian Ambassador to Kenya's card and explained that I wished to get a visa but it had to be granted quickly as I was going to an important medical meeting in Bali later that day to which I was to present a paper (partially true).

He looked at me, smiled and said "All these people going to important meeting, not possible to get visa today."

I was overcome with disappointment and pleaded, "But the ambassador promised me that I would get a visa quickly."

He smiled at me and said "wait".

He then went through the door behind him and after awhile he explained that his boss wanted to see me but that meant that I would have to offer him something for his efforts.

Coming from Africa, I was accustomed to all different types of bribes and I recognized this one. I asked him how much. He explained that his boss had a large family and needed school fees and uniforms. I offered him $50 US and he smiled, went back through the door, and invited me into a bleak room where a tired official sat behind another desk.

This one explained, "My clerk said that you offered me $50 US to help you to get a visa. I very much appreciate this but I can only accept it if you can assure me that it comes from the bottom of your heart."

I took his hand, kissed it and soulfully replied, "It does, sir, from the bottom of my heart".

I grabbed the visas and ran back to Margaret to catch the aircraft to Jakarta then to Bali.

Soon we were in Bali. We were shown to a modest cabin on stilts over the beach. That night, I took my prepared paper to the conference hall. I was to speak on the awful, needless loss of children in Africa from preventable diseases. I had many slides and accurate figures. On arrival in the hall I was told that my presentation had been cancelled to allow the US delegate from a generous donor group to present a paper on health care in the inner cities of the east coast of the United States. She had a boring presentation filled with statistically significant numbers demonstrating that the poor children in these areas did not have money and that people with no money tend to get sick and that when poor people get sick they often die. I am familiar with this type of pseudo-logic and I continue to witness its presentation in various forms to this day. I was pissed off with being replaced by this powerful and ever-overwhelming force.

I went back to my cabin to receive an invitation from my friend Martin Scheel, who had been a missionary in India for many years and on his return to Germany had assumed the leadership of DIFAEM (the German Institute for Medical Missions) in Tubingen. Martin had been a good friend over the years and we shared similar views over the health care offered by medical missions.

Martin knew of the problems my daughter Judy's problems which she was experiencing with her type 1 diabetes. She had been diagnosed with it when she was four years old, on Christmas Eve in Dar es Salaam. Judy was being controlled by subcutaneous insulin in accordance with her urinary sugars, an ancient and inappropriate method. Martin assured me that Judy needed to be managed in the first class juvenile diabetes unit in Ulm, Germany. He assured me that he would find funding for this, so I took Judy with her sister Patricia to Ulm for an in-house assessment and management course lasting about one week. This did help her for awhile, but she was now in her early teens and not very compliant with the necessary routines.

In Bali, Martin and I sat on the veranda of his cabin and we had a good time reminiscing about the various CMC activities in which we had been involved and planning our own world-shaking programs to improve the disastrous picture of health care in the third world. We almost finished a bottle of fine whiskey and I stumbled over to our cabin to find Margaret asleep, fortunately.

We flew from Bali to Hong Kong and prepared for Margaret's round-the-world anniversary tour. We booked into the lovely Peninsula Hotel in Hong Kong where I had stayed previously and the service and setting were impressive. We had a room high up with a lovely view of the sea and its surrounding magnificent buildings. I ordered a room service breakfast served by a superb staff who even offered to butter our rolls. We were introduced to the delicious breakfast dish, chicken porridge. We ventured into the formidable shopping area of Hong Kong, small streets running into even smaller alleyways, all with an abundance of goods in full view. We settled on a superb set of luggage which we really needed.

That evening I awoke with a jet lag hangover and Margaret was fast asleep. I went into the streets to visit the shops which were still open. I saw a collection of wrist watches including a top of the line Rolex for the very low price of $20.

I had been warned about this so I asked the vendor, "How do I know if this is really a Rolex?"

He smiled at me and said "You never know, do one?"

I bought it and have kept it to this day.

Marg and I went to the airport the next day and I took her to the departure gate. I looked through my wallet and found a few extra US dollars so I gave them to her to augment the cache of traveller's cheques she had. She resisted for awhile but I explained that I had a direct flight from Hong Kong to Nairobi via Bombay which would take me only a few hours and I should be home by midnight, so she reluctantly took my few hundred dollars and I kissed her goodbye.

I had a pleasant flight to Bombay aboard Cathay Pacific which was well-staffed and luxurious. On landing in Bombay I noticed an old Ethiopian lady who was having great difficulty reaching the terminal so I stayed behind to help her. She was going to Nairobi also, on her way to Addis Ababa so I assisted her to make all these connections. In so doing, I lost my place in the Nairobi-bound line and was last up to the desk. A Kenya Airways clerk looked at my ticket and told me that I could not board that flight but I would have to wait for the next flight which was in one week's time. I tried my best to convince him that I had a confirmed ticket so I could not be summarily bumped. It was to no avail. I even explained that I was one of the Kenya Airways medical staff, also to no avail. Just then I spotted the entire Kenya Airways flight crew coming through the airport to board their aircraft. I recognized the pilot, a man whose family I had treated many times. I jumped up and down shouting his name hoping that I would be heard over the plexiglass partitions. But he did not hear me, and afterwards I saw the aircraft taking off for Nairobi.

I was alone in the Bombay airport with no money except for a $5 US bill I had retained. I sat down with my bags and wondered what I should do next. Repeated pleading at the Kenya Airways counter was to no avail. I even went to the Kenya Airways station manager and desperately requested his help. He laughed at me and, in derision, told me "You just have to wait till next week!"

As the day went by I realized that I had not eaten but thankfully I was able to drink from a water fountain nearby. That night as I sat with my bags a cleaning woman approached me and roughly squished her mop over my bag.

I asked her not to do that and she laughed at me and replied "I can do anything, I am untouchable."

That drove home to me the wickedness of the caste system. I secured my bags under me and tried to go to sleep unsuccessfully. As the sun rose I realized that I could not survive in this way so I did some intense planning. I remembered that I did know someone in Bombay and I would try to contact her. Bunty had been one of my residents in pediatrics at McGill. She had married a wealthy Parsee in Bombay and settled there. I found her address and phone number in my little black book. I decided to leave the airport and seek her. I walked out of the front door to be greeted by a host of hustling bustling taxi drivers who offered me cheap prices to take me into town.

A Sikh man with a kind face between his turban and his beard assured me that he would look after me as I appeared to be lost. I told him that I wanted to go to a reasonable hotel with a telephone. He drove me around and eventually dropped me at a seedy-looking house which doubled as a hotel. I asked him the fare and he told me $20 US. I shouted and told him that I could only afford $2; he grudgingly accepted that. That took the greater part of the day yet without food. I went to bed and early in the morning I went to the front desk and called Bunty's number.

"Hello," I heard.

I replied "I want to speak to Bunty Bains from Canada. I am Dr Colin Forbes."

"Hi Colin," she interrupted, "what are you doing here?"

I explained where I was and she was shocked. Apparently it was in one of the most dangerous parts of the city. She advised me not to move and to wait for her. Shortly afterwards she arrived in one of Bombay's ubiquitous maxis with her driver. She settled my hotel bill and we drove off into a different world, one of large luxurious homes in pleasant tree-lined roads.

Bunty explained that her husband's family were not pleased with her and she was having a difficult time settling into life in India. Her husband arrived and learned about my plight. His parents owned, amongst many other things, a travel agency so he quickly arranged a flight back to Nairobi via Air India that night in first class. He took us out for a real Indian dinner and took me to the airport. Bunty lent me $120 in case there were any more problems. I promised to pay her back. Years later she reminded me of this and I quickly reimbursed her. In the first class cabin I was showered with Air India largesse. I was downing my second champagne when the passenger next to me started chatting about his life. He explained that he was working for an oil firm in Calgary and was just returning from a business trip to Saudi Arabia. He explained that his business in Calgary could make a million dollars a day in the deal in which he had just completed in Abu Dhabi. He gave me his business card and urged me to look him up sometimes if I was ever in Calgary. I never did.

Back in Nairobi I was extremely upset at the treatment given to me by Kenya Airways in Bombay. I approached the management about it but I was told there was little I could do about it. Bombay–Nairobi was an extremely busy route and to assure a seat one would have to bribe the station master handsomely.

I managed to obtain a post as pediatrician to Kenya Airways and to retain it for quite a few years until the new generation of African Kenyan pediatricians successfully dislodged me from that job. They explained that they could not agree with such a sought-after post being given to a foreigner like Forbes.

That reverse racism would rapidly take its hold in all areas of Kenyan society and qualified, efficient personnel, expatriate, white or Indian-Kenyan, would be unceremoniously ejected from their post by scheming, tribally connected Africans on their way up on the gravy train. Fortunately there was a backbone of bright, intelligent, honest and hard-working African doctors who managed to stick to the high principles we had developed in the Department of Pediatrics led by Professor Alan Ross from McGill. He carefully chose talented Kenyan leaders to go to McGill for further post-graduate training and on return they gradually replaced all the expatriates who returned home. Except for me, who opted to remain in Kenya.

Chapter Twenty

FAMILY HOLIDAYS

Our children had all left Kenya for further education overseas: Heather in the USA and Canada, George in Switzerland, England and Canada, Patricia in Canada and the USA, Judy in Canada and the US, and Carl in the UK and Canada. We tried our best to bring them back for Christmas holidays and inevitably they arrived with a succession of soul-mates. Christmas is traditionally a time when the well-to-do in Kenya leave Nairobi and head to the coast. This was a 10-hour journey for us, through the Kamba jungles then about halfway a must-do pit stop on reaching the plains at Mtito Andei for the entire 8 to 14 inhabitants of the Volkswagen Kombi where we all converged on the food shop and loaded up on meat samosas, kebabs and coconut water for the last half of our journey.

This second half included a stretch through one of Kenya's famous game parks, Tsavo. Invariably we would have to stop to allow a herd of elephants to leisurely cross the road. A Canadian friend, Dr Harry Miller, who was also a pilot working with the Flying Doctors, had a Porsche which he drove at breakneck speeds on the road through Tsavo. He boasted that on one of these trips he was faced with a giraffe slowly crossing the road and he had no option but to drive between its legs under its belly to safety on the other side. I took this story with a grain of salt and another shot of rum.

One could not miss the approach to Mombasa as it traversed a causeway leading to the island. Nearby was the local abattoir with accompanying smells. By then all the Kombi passengers would be asleep except one—Patricia. She invariably would ask "Where's Mombasa, Dad?" and without words I would point ahead.

She loved that ritual because it meant that once we cleared the bustle of steaming Mombasa we were heading to the Ukunda ferry to take us off the island and onto the south coast. Waiting for the ferry was a unique experience. We would be surrounded by a host of beggars—mostly lepers with horrible facial deformities, usually blind, and led by pleading little children, and polio victims dragging their useless legs up to the van. Who could resist giving our paltry sums of money to these unfortunates? We couldn't! The welcoming group were the little children selling peanuts and cashew nuts, which we eagerly devoured as we drove down the one-lane road to Diani Beach.

Our resting place in Diani, at first, was usually our tents. We certainly could not afford the classy hotels there. Pitching a tent on the beach was an enjoyable family and friends' effort, and after a quickly produced evening meal we would all fall asleep. One night as I was carrying out my usual inspection of the tent I was horrified to see one end of it being slashed open by a large cutlass (*panga*). I screamed "*Mwizi, lete bunduki*" (thief, get the gun!). We had no gun but that was enough to send the two thieves dashing off. I tried to follow them but it was impossible for me to even walk over the sharp coral over which they sped barefooted. We then arranged a guard system, which really didn't work as the appointed guard invariably fell asleep under the Indian Ocean night sky.

My son Carl had grown into a tall, handsome young man so he was usually accompanied on his holiday by a female classmate from Canada. Carl had a significant eating disorder—he hated vegetables, especially carrots. His mother's meal song was "Carl, eat your carrots!" and we usually joined in the chorus.

His current beau was an intense, attentive Canadian lass from his class at the University of Calgary. She did her best to demonstrate her affection for Carl and to attend to his every need. We were having a glorious meal on the beach which Margaret and I had prepared. Of course Carl polished off everything on his plate except the carrots.

His girlfriend shouted "Carl, eat your carrots!"

The entire Forbes family looked at each other and then uncontrollably burst into raucous laughter, repeating the well-known refrain. We did our best to excuse our behaviour but that particular lass did not come back the following year.

One memorable year our eldest daughter, Heather, came for the holidays with her boyfriend, Steve. He was the only son of an immigrant Jewish Montreal family. Heather and Steve travelled to Kenya via Israel to gain our blessing on their impending engagement. Steve had been accepted into medical school at McGill and this was his final trip abroad before starting his studies. We were overjoyed as the two were so obviously in love. Heather decided to take Steve down to the coast so I lent them my car as she was an expert driver. Her brother George went with them. On their return George had a problem with the car so Heather and Steve decided to accept the offer of a drive back to Nairobi with a Canadian family whom they met at the coast. On the way back, with all passengers asleep, the Canadian lady who was driving lost control of the car and a horrible crash ensued. A passing motorist took all the injured to a local hospital. Steve died, as did one of the Canadian family's daughters. Heather was severely bruised. My Danish surgeon friend, Tom Jorgensen, himself a Flying Doctor, arranged Heather's immediate transfer by air to Nairobi.

She did not know of Steve's death. We told her the next morning and she was devastated. I also informed Steve's family in Montreal and they immediately laid the blame on Heather. The next days were busy ones for me. I arranged the transfer of Steve's body to Nairobi and contacted the local Jewish synagogue who then took the responsibility of carrying out the rigidly required religious ceremonies. As it was a fatal road accident, the

Kenyan police demanded an autopsy. The rabbi informed me that this was not acceptable. I explained this to the government pathologist who agreed to forgo the formal autopsy and provided me with a false certificate that afternoon. On my return to the morgue to collect the body the pathologist explained that he would need money for the kind service he offered me. I willingly gave him a few thousand shillings, loaded Steve's body into a rented truck and took it to the synagogue. There they informed me that a full autopsy had indeed been done and that Steve died of a ruptured spleen—a death that could have been prevented with proper management.

The Jewish tradition is that burial must be as quickly as possible after death so I arranged for a flight back to Montreal that night. Heather insisted on accompanying Steve's body, so she did, covered in bandages and loaded with pain-relief pills. I clearly remember walking Heather up the stairs to the aircraft with George's support, getting her settled, then handing her over to the kind and attentive Kenya Airways staff. Heather arrived safely in Montreal to be greeted by a grieving, accusing family. The Jewish ritual of "sitting shiva" commenced and for the next eight days Heather sat in a corner of a room with grieving relatives and friends, some of whom walked by her and pretended to spit on her. That experience shook Heather to the core. In penance, she officially converted to Judaism and remains a Jew to this day.

Her brother George, by his own brilliance, gained admission to medical school at McGill after completing a bachelor's degree in computer science. He told us that he would marry a Norwegian fellow student at McGill who had also been brought up in Kenya. Her parents were architects serving in Africa under the Norwegian government program. So we arranged a marriage in Nairobi which I gladly sponsored. It was to be a sumptuous affair in the Catholic university chapel followed by a grand reception at our delightful home in the Kitisuru suburb in Nairobi. The arrangements for the wedding were made at many evening meetings in our home, attended by the entire wedding party including the bride's parents. We decided to arrange every detail—the transport, church service, wedding feast, speeches, entertainment and honeymoon departure with accompanying vehicle noises and decorations. These planning meetings were great fun and I provided a never-ending supply of Jamaican rum. There was great hilarity but after awhile we noticed that her parents seemed puzzled and not particularly in agreement with all the loud levity. We fed them more rum and cigarettes and that seemed to do the trick.

A couple years later George and his wife returned to Nairobi for a summer holiday. They brought with them a group of their university friends, at my expense. We did have a problem housing them all so initially we had to place five, three females and two males, in one large room. The next morning George went into the room to find his new wife sharing a sleeping bag with a mutual friend from McGill, where he was an associate professor. This did not go over well with George and on their return he smartly separated from his wife. Our next visit from George was a few Christmases later. This time he brought a fellow student—a black woman. He proudly announced that she was the daughter of a well-known West Indian activist who was one of the leaders of an uprising at Sir George Williams College that destroyed the new computer department. It was evident that George's attitude had changed considerably. He was now an ardent black power activist. He explained that the black people would have to regain the power they had lost through centuries of slavery, Jim Crow and persistent racism. I recognized that I shared many of his beliefs and aspirations but as a devout follower of Gandhi and Martin Luther King I believed that our aspirations could be gained in a nonviolent way.

As usual, we went to the coast for our Christmas holidays. By then, Margaret and I were deeply involved in purchasing a half share in the 10-cottage complex called Warandale where we had spent many holidays. We decided to buy it from an English architect developer in a 50/50 deal with a Danish architect called Finn and his wife Clara. We took a particularly beautiful beachfront cottage and housed our large family group. We gave George and his girlfriend a room upstairs. The next morning, Christmas Day, we all gathered for our breakfast lovingly and expertly prepared and served by our devoted African staff. George started a rant which was to last all day with disastrous results. He accused us of giving him what in Canada hotel parlance was called the "elevator room"—one beside the noisy elevator and so the least desirable. Christmas dinner preparation started early and we all took our places in and around the kitchen and dining room at our allotted and chosen tasks. Patricia was dressed as usual in a coastal wrap-around called a *kikoi*. George's girlfriend was dressed in a skimpy bikini.

Patricia busily passed her in the kitchen and said "Hey, you're a jungle bunny!"

At that time the saying was apparently a derogatory one used to describe black women. George immediately accosted her, menacingly shook his finger in her face and said "Don't ever speak to my friend like that again".

Patricia burst into tears and retreated into her bedroom where she spent the rest of the holidays.

That Christmas dinner was a tragic one. Margaret and I did our best to offer true family hospitality to all our children and their friends. The wine and the rum flowed freely so it was not surprising that George soon got particularly belligerent. He expounded on the black power movement and excused me of paying more attention to my Scottish ancestry than to my African roots.

I objected to this and he shouted at me "Look, you married a white woman!" He pointed at Margaret and growled "She's white trash!"

I was angry and was confused as to what response I could make. Immediately our son Carl drew up to his full six feet, stepped over to George and threw a measured heavy punch in his face.

George was stunned and immediately said "You have assaulted me. I am going to bring you up to the police!"

I attempted to make peace between my sons but George took his girlfriend to his cottage. I did not know how to proceed so I went over to George's cottage and saw him sitting outside flicking his cigarette lighter as if to set the thatch roof on fire. I urged him to settle down but he insisted on taking Carl to the police. We all drove up to the Ukunda police station. There we were greeted by a Christmas-liquor-soaked policeman who incongruously heard our story and insisted that as this was a family quarrel, we should go home and sleep it off. George refused so we spent the rest of the night at the police station painstakingly reciting our stories taken down laboriously in long-hand on many sheets of foolscap paper. George and his friend left us the next morning and we last saw them walking along the beach on the way to Mombasa. Sometime later I was contacted by George's girlfriend, who tried to rationalize his increasingly aggressive and inexplicable behaviour fueled by alcohol. It had caused her to leave him but she was very worried about him.

After much discussion with my medical friends we decided that it was best for me to report George to the College of Physicians and Surgeons of Canada and to explain that he was an impaired doctor needing the help that was provided in these cases. Fortunately the medical authorities took quick action. He lost his licence to practise and was ordered to attend a facility for such impaired doctors in Ontario for a period of three months. They were able to offer him expert care to wean him off his addictions and to deal with his professional life. Shortly after, I received a letter from George explaining his recovery. He blamed me for his problems as I was myself an alcoholic, endangering the lives of my patients and he wanted nothing more to do with me or with any other members of the family. To this day I have had no contact with George. Fortunately his mother has seen fit to forgive him for his behaviour and only wishes that he would "come back to me".

Chapter Twenty-one

PAT AND PUNKIE

Patricia recovered from her devastating ordeal at the coast. She returned to the USA and continued her career as in international model and a partner in her husband's hair salon. Luke was an accomplished hair stylist serving the upper echelons of black American society. Unfortunately he was also an alcoholic and a drug user who dragged Patricia down that devastating road. He was also abusive to her, accusing her of not being black enough, and so forth. They did get married and Pat then became pregnant. Fortunately, partly due to her exposure to my rants on the effects of drugs and alcohol on pregnant women, she immediately stopped using them. One day, Patricia phoned and informed us of her impending delivery. She asked Margaret to come to be with her. We recognized this as an important plea so within 24 hours Margaret was on her way from Africa to New Jersey, just in time to welcome Patricia home with her new baby. Pat pleaded with Marg to help her get her baby away from Luke and to join us in Nairobi. She told her a horror story of Luke's inhumane treatment and his drug-induced wild behaviour with his newborn. Marg and Pat packed up wildly and one morning after Luke had left for work they called a cab and took off with her three-week-old baby to fly to Montreal where they miraculously obtained an American passport for the virtually kidnapped baby. After a night at Heather's home, they flew to London to my sister Norma's home in Rickmansworth and her husband, John, drove them to Heathrow for the long flight to Africa.

At the Nairobi airport I joined the sweating, pushing crowd to welcome the Kenya Airways plane from London. I eventually spotted my wife pushing a trolley full of bags and a tired, pale Patricia struggling behind her, wearing what appeared to be a chest bandage. I greeted her warmly and she opened the shoulder bag to reveal a screaming, wiggling little worm-like creature—her daughter.

"She's yours, Daddy!" she cried.

"No Pat, she's ours and we will all look after her."

Her name was Christine Noel, born on Christmas Eve, and she quickly took control of all our lives. I rapidly became a substitute father and I loved that role. I swore to myself that I would do a better job with her than I had done with my own children. Patricia was an expert breastfeeder but, having given up her alcohol and drugs, she was still addicted to cigarettes.

We could not help but note that baby Chris had her periods of what seemed to be extreme discomfort, screaming and wrestling. The attacks usually happened at about 2-3 am and were disturbing to the entire household. To give Patricia a much-needed rest, I took over the comforting role on the early morning fussing periods. We all agreed that they were a form of three-month colic which plagued some babies for no apparent reason. My unique routine was to cuddle the screaming bundle on my shoulder, kissing her repeatedly, then dancing slowly around the living room to the soft strains of "Cherish" by Kool and the Gang. Gradually she would settle down then go off to sleep. All that took about an hour so I would quickly dash back into bed to get some sleep before my early morning hospital rounds. After awhile I realized that these screaming attacks were not colic but a nicotine withdrawal reaction. Pat and I had some serious talks and she eventually gave up smoking, which dramatically improved Chris's behaviour. Chris had a beautiful baby face with full cheeks and prominent lips. I spent a lot of time gazing into her face and one day I said to myself she has a punkie face so I called her Punkie and that is what I call her to this day, 25 years later.

Chapter Twenty-two

HOME ON TATE CLOSE

Our home was on Tate Close, a branch at the end of Kitisuru Road, part of an estate that was a collection of imposing houses, home to some embassies and many wealthy foreigners and Africans. Our little road was lined with jacaranda trees and at the appropriate time annually their purple flowers would cover the entire road so I drove home over a purple carpet. Our three-acre plot extended down a sloping hill to the river. It contained a forest of eucalyptus trees whose gentle swaying welcomed my early mornings. A great variety of birds, mostly small finches and thrushes, visited our veranda every morning. I eventually decided to feed them seeds in a number of large trays which I secured along the wall of the veranda. There followed a host of activity with hundreds of cute little birds fighting their way for the seeds. Inevitably, some strange-looking birds with bright yellow crowns, red breasts and very long tails would swoop down, whoosh the finches away with their long tails and settle down to gorge on a breakfast of their own. These were pin-tailed wydahs. This scene fascinated me and I spent many precious early morning moments watching the beautiful spectacle. Many other birds dropped by—eagles, owls and turacos. Other wildlife traversed our property—a family of small antelopes called dikdiks lived nearby and were often chased by the dogs of the area.

Much-feared and menacing snakes sometimes made their appearance. The shout of *NYOKA* (snake) would cause consternation to all of our African staff and all of us. The more agile would run after the creatures with snake sticks—tree branches with a Y end which would be used to immobilize the snake's head until the relentless beating and stoning would take the life of the creature. Proudly, the staff member would demonstrate the result of his prowess to me awaiting the expected reward, usually at least 20 shillings. Once we had an increased number of snakes, reported to be killing the chickens of the area. We were unsure about the safety of this situation as some of the snakes (a minority) were poisonous. I offered a bounty of 20 shillings for every dead snake. Soon my gardener, a scheming, wily old man, presented me with a bag of 20 snakes. I was shocked, as 400 shillings at that time was a handsome sum. Anyhow I paid.

Punkie's first birthday party was a memorable affair. Among the guests were our new friends Charles and Margaret Njonjo and their children.

Margaret and Punkie.

Charles had convinced me to become a Kenyan citizen. He explained that life would become easier and more profitable for me. I went through the necessary procedures and reached the final stage—the renunciation of my Canadian passport. I consulted the Canadian High Commission about this and they explained that Canada had no problem with dual citizenship but the Kenyans certainly did not allow it. So I must make the choice. I dutifully filled out the renunciation papers and presented them to the Canadians who accepted them with due warnings (nudge, nudge, wink, wink) that I would have to re-apply if I ever wanted to become a Canadian again. Some months later, I was visited in my office by a senior French Canadian diplomat whose children I had looked after. He explained that he was returning to Canada and on clearing out his desk he had discovered my passport. He handed it over to me after thanking me for caring for his children. He said, "Come see me in Montreal, we will have a Molson's together." I thanked him profusely as I regained my dual citizenship, soon to become two of the four citizenships I currently hold: Canadian, Kenyan, Jamaican and British (in dispute).

My Kenyan citizenship did help me to obtain several posts, such as the Kenya Airways one, pediatrician to the family of president Moi, professor at the medical school, and many other goodies. Increasingly, such posts were being nationalized. This was an attempt by the nation to gain its full place in the running of its affairs—an admirable effort but one that resulted in many instances of reversed racism. I learned this the hard way. For example, at the university I was still required to give lectures, but only at 7:30 am, a time when no African lecturers were available. I did this with pleasure and to my joy, these very early morning lectures were fully attended. However, Kenyan citizenship did not always work to my advantage.

Once I was proud to discover an additional way of diagnosing malaria. That common disease was noted for its missed or false diagnosis. Any fever in a child from western or coastal Kenya was deemed to be malaria, often with disastrous consequences—death from malaria that had been treated as pneumonia, meningitis or other forms of sepsis. The weak excuse was usually that the malaria slide was negative so it could not be malaria. In many cases the smear was negative because the child had received an initial dose of an anti-malarial medication which eradicated the circulating form of the parasite and caused it to be undetected in a blood smear.

I noticed that in malarious patients the blood count analysis that invariably accompanied the smear always produced a lower platelet count. Normally this count is somewhere above 200,000 but in all malaria cases it was invariably much lower, in the region of 50,000 or less. Since the platelet count was an integral part of the Coulter counter readout it was always available and reasonably reliable. I then surmised that this low platelet count (thrombocytopenia) could be used as a valuable tool in diagnosing difficult cases of malaria. I used this to great advantage in many cases. Once a set of twins were brought to me by a neighbour. They had been increasingly ill for several days on their return from a holiday at the coast. They were investigated and treated by a number of doctors who categorically stated that they did not have malaria as their blood smears were negative. When I saw them they were ill, confused, feverish and near death. A rapid blood test revealed marked thrombocytopenia but negative malaria parasites. Of course they had received anti-malarial prophylaxis while at the coast. I diagnosed near cerebral malaria and proceeded to administer the most appropriate medicine. At that time this was a Chinese herbal medication—*quing qua cho,* whose active ingredient was artemisinin.

The Americans refused to license this drug for about 10 years and used a preparation called mefloquin, which had psychotrophic effects and variable anti-malarial effectivity. I injected the artemisinin into the lads freely. They improved rapidly. I was most impressed by my discovery of a reliable method of diagnosing malaria so I decided to do a proper study to prove my hypothesis. Two female students in their final year had asked me if I had any work they could do as part of their final year extra-curricular activities. I challenged them with my hypothesis about the malaria diagnosis. They quickly accepted the challenge and we drew up a proposal and methodology, which they outlined with remarkable accuracy and relevance. Shortly we completed the study with a more-than-necessary study size, wrote it up and were ready to publish it. We presented it to the university for their routine approval. I received a letter from their department stating that this study could not be published as it was done without university approval. The dean explained that the university no longer allowed "foreigners" to conduct medical research in their medical school. The dean (an Indian female who had been one of my students) was adamant when I tried to explain my objection to her disapproval. "Fuck me," I thought, and that began my process of disassociating myself from Kenyan academic society. A series of other misadventures followed, all playing part in my eventual decision to leave Africa.

Gertrude's Garden Children's Hospital is one of the most appealing children's hospitals in the world. It is set in 13 acres of lush tropical land in Nairobi's most exclusive community, Muthaiga. Popular knowledge is that it was commissioned by an extremely wealthy Nairobi resident, once the mayor and also an extremely successful businessman, mostly in real estate. Colonel Grogan was a veteran who settled in Kenya after the Second World War. He fell madly in love with a local British beauty named Gertrude and wanted to marry her. Her parents were not too crazy about the situation as they disapproved of the reputation that Colonel Grogan had. The colonel then challenged Gertrude's parents, promising to walk from Cape to Cairo if he could gain her hand in marriage. He set about doing this daunting task and completed it, thus winning Gertrude.

Unfortunately shortly after their marriage, Gertrude died during child birth. Devastated, the colonel decided to create a memorial for her. There were a number of white children orphaned due to the war so he built a home for them on part of his extensive property in Muthaiga and insisted on calling it Gertrude's Garden. After awhile it morphed into a hospital for white children. The primary pediatrician at that time in Nairobi was Dr Patience Davis. She enlisted the help of an English nurse, Matron Felicity Fenwick. Together they created an efficient and well-run children's hospital. Soon after independence it was obvious that this hospital could not function on its racial bias so African children were also admitted.

They were in two groups—the children of the now-wealthy African upper class and a group of children who occupied a dormitory downstairs, patients of an English ENT government surgeon who had been in his ward at Kenyatta Hospital suffering from a strange malignancy which caused a recognizable swelling of the face. Much work had been done on this tumour by a brilliant surgeon in Mulago Hospital in Kampala, Dr Dennis Burkitt. He mapped its spread across East Africa and postulated a relationship with malaria and a virus called Epstein Barr, the same one now recognized as the cause of infectious mononucleosis. His theory was that the EB virus in children whose immune system was primed by malaria could be a factor in producing this malignancy, later to be called Burkitt's lymphoma.

I once attended a memorable lecture by Dennis Burkitt. It was jokingly advertised as "Up the Nile with Dennis Burkitt". Burkitt himself was a missionary doctor and an ardent Christian. He was earnest about his work and became involved in devising a method of chemo- and radio-therapy that resulted in saving many African children's lives. He excitingly explained his theory about the spread of the disease, following malaria up the Nile. He pointed this out with a number of impressive slides; on one slide change, his excitement overcame him—and lo and behold, his entire set of full dentures flew out of his mouth. We patiently waited until he recovered them from the floor, washed them in the lab sink on his desk, and deftly replaced them with a "Dear me, so sorry".

I was invited by Dr Patience Davis to take up a post at Gertrude's Garden. I did this gladly and soon I was admitting patients to this wonderful facility. I also gave my service free of charge to the African children downstairs.

After awhile, Patience Davis left Kenya and I was the de facto senior pediatrician at Gertrude's. I quickly encouraged young pediatricians, mostly my former African students, to join the staff. I installed a medical advisory council to look after the professional aspects of the hospital and I instituted a series of regular clinical meetings, sometimes hosted by a pharmaceutical company that would provide samosas, sandwiches and the occasional wine. These were exciting times as I could see the emergence of a cadre of bright, energetic young pediatricians whose common base was Gertrude's. The hospital was overseen by a board of governors as set up by Colonel Grogan. The board was made up of a group of aging white men who appointed an administrator to be full time at the hospital and to run the entire non-medical aspect of such an important and ever-growing institution. Inevitably, the hospital superintendent was also a senior white man. For some time he was a retired soldier, Colonel Harper. He was known to like his liquor. He passed away and had to be replaced. One of the board members was Eddie Hollister, an ex-RAF Battle of Britain pilot who told us of a young retired British major who was interested in the post of administrator of Gertrude's hospital. We eagerly interviewed him. Arthur Brown was a mid-career affable man who thought highly of himself and was eager to obtain this plum posting in one of the few neo-colonial institutions left in Africa. Eddie had also invited me to become a member of the board of governors.

Arthur took over the entire hospital, making decisions unilaterally with reckless abandon to be questioned by no one. After awhile I recognized the danger of this situation and I feared that what we had so successfully built up over the years was in danger of being converted into a one-man show. I sought desperately to address the situation and to limit the powers of Arthur Brown, preferably to get him fired. I wrote many reports and complaints and appeared before many decision makers in my attempt to stem the Brown regime. In many of these attempts I enlisted my recently enrolled junior partner, Dr Cecil Manley (more on him later). Eventually the board of governors, including Eddie Hollister, who with his delightful wife Berit were now good friends of mine, all saw things my way and we dismissed Arthur with handsome parting perks. In a brave move we appointed a senior African nurse, British trained, to take over the post of administrator. Sister Doris Bulwa came to this post with much hope and support, but she was unable to do the job properly. She became heavily involved in tribal politics and soon this caused disquiet among the staff and she too had to be let go. We then advertised locally for an administrator and fortunately we were able to secure the services of a brilliant Luo manager whose wise guidance and expertise were able to rescue Gertrude's from impending disaster.

YOUNG PARTNERS

As my practice grew it became evident that I would need help to keep up with the ever-increasing demands on my time and skill. I did have a number of young doctors, mostly my past students, whom I invited to be part of my team. Their duties included taking off-duty hours on call, assisting me in clinics during the day and covering me when I was away on holidays or on overseas appointments. The first of these was a young Indian doctor, Dr Surya Shah. He was a well-trained graduate of Makerere University who had done post-graduate training in pediatric cardiology. He was hard working, conscientious and loyal. He kept his post as a lecturer in the Department of Pediatrics at the university but got increasingly involved in my practice. In 1982 Kenya had a surprise political-tribal-racial uprising. Violent rioting in Nairobi focussed on the Indian community. Stores were looted, Indian homes attacked and a surprising number of Indian women were reported to have been raped. For weeks after, the greeting from an Indian friend was "___ was raped you know".

My involvement was a report from a despondent, discouraged Surya the morning after the riot. He described that as he was driving home from my office that night he was attacked by an angry mob. They ordered him out of his car, told him to lie down, and gave him a few kicks and blows. They stole his money then they left him. On his arrival at home he found his family locked in their home, paralysed with fear.

"That's it, Colin," he told me, "we're leaving."

He urged me to help him escape. I promised to do so and we drew up several plans for him and his family to escape to Canada. I wrote many letters to Canada explaining Surya's predicament and extolling his virtues. He eventually went to Saskatchewan where he was forced to retake his examinations and redo the entire punitive programs through which the Canadian medical colleges put foreign medical graduates. Surya's wife was also a pediatrician but she stayed at home and supported their children while Surya went through his exhaustive duties. He regained his medical degrees and continued in his cardiology sub-specialty. He eventually went to Newfoundland where he still continues his admirable work.

Many other young doctors were employed in my busy practice. They included Ed Kasirye, a brilliant Ugandan pediatrician, a refugee from Idi Amin's terror regime especially against the Baganda. He was a lecturer at the University of Nairobi and willingly joined my practice part time. His smiling, supportive, expert performance was most welcome. He is now a leading pediatrician in his home town, Kampala, happily married with two children. I also had a succession of foreign graduates coming to do their Africa time with me in my practice. They included many English, American and mostly Canadian doctors. I did as much as I could to help them understand the principles of practising pediatrics under limited conditions and scarce resources. Wherever possible I took them with me to my "bush clinics".

One day I was visited by a young doctor who asked me if I could assist him. He was Cecil Manley, son of a colleague of mine, Dr Tim Manley, a successful family practitioner in Nairobi. Tim was of a mixed-race Kikuyu and white family; his sister was the nurse at a large children's hospital in Nairobi which I served. Cecil had graduated in medicine in Ireland and did post-graduate work in pediatrics there. On his return to Kenya he was working as a pediatrician at the newly born ward of the city council hospital, a basic institution with limited resources. I was impressed by Cecil's qualifications and experience and gladly welcomed him into my practice. I had him accompany me on my ward rounds at Gertrude's and assist me in my private practice. I quickly brought him on board as a partner and we agreed on a 50/50 split of our earnings and sharing holiday duties and out-of-hours work. I took full advantage of this as the senior partner and it seemed to be mutually beneficial. At that time Cecil became interested in a program called PALS (Pediatric Advanced Life Support), a highly organized program offering courses and diplomas. I admired Cecil's enthusiasm and noted that it occupied an increasing amount of his time and several overseas trips. Nevertheless, I covered on his trips and he also looked after my patients when I was away. He soon began to complain about the amount of work he was being forced to do and suggested that a 50/50 split was unreasonable as he was doing more work than I was.

I agonized about this for some time but the final straw came one day when I was examining a patient of mine and his mother said "Dr Forbes, I am so glad to see you back in practice".

"Why do you say that?" I asked.

"Well, as you know," she replied "the word is that you are sick with approaching Alzheimer's and you are going to retire—that's what Dr Manley says."

"Fuck me," I said to myself again, "that little bastard is screwing up my life."

One Sunday, after days of agonizing, I decided to leave the practice as I didn't want to have anything to do with that little weasel again. I went to my office in Gertrude's and started to pack up all my personal belongings. I called Cecil and told him what I was doing and told him to come over if he wanted to witness it. He rushed over and seemed surprised. I explained my reasons and continued to pack up my whole life's work that afternoon. I tried my best to keep from losing my temper.

Aminah, Cecil's new wife, appeared. She was the daughter of a prominent Ismaili family. Cecil had courted her for some time, often sharing with me his ambivalence towards their relationship. His marriage was a social event of the year. I even graced the event with a tap dance with my then dancing partner, the doctor of the Canadian High Commission.

Tap dancing at Cecil's wedding.

Aminah barged in, saw what I was doing, then started her diatribe.

"How dare you!" she shouted. "After all that Cecil has done for you? Covering your off-duty hours and trips and getting only 50 per cent of your earnings. You should be giving him much more."

"Stop," I shouted. "What right do you have to come into my office at this most important time of my life and spit in my face!"

She quieted and I completed my packing and walked out, never again to return to Gertrude's Garden Children's Hospital. Cecil Manley took over my practice and my place on the hospital governing board, so I was virtually excommunicated from the medical community in Nairobi.

Chapter Twenty-three

KITISURU AND PERSONAL CHALLENGES

Those were difficult days, not only for me but also for my family. We were essentially an empty nest home. Most of our children were away. We had occasional holiday visits which we enjoyed but Christmas always bore the memories of the disastrous time at the coast with George's meltdown. But all was not quiet at our Kitisuru home. Ever so frequently we had break-ins from thieves who came up from the river, cut the fence and entered our living room through the windows. They usually took our electronics, TVs, music systems and the contents of my liquor cabinet. We regarded them as benign intruders on our privacy and took appropriate measures to protect ourselves from further attack. Our friend Betty Mbaka, who had experienced several such intrusions, recommended an artisan (*fundi*) who would provide a system of break-in-proof protections. The *fundi* was a Sikh gentleman, Mr Singh, who erected bars on our windows and created a massive system of retractable metal gates covering our glass doors.

One night Marg and I were awakened by a loud noise—gun shots, screams, breaking glass and falling metal. I looked out of my upstairs bedroom window to see a gang of about 16 men swarming over the property from the river fence. Some of them were directly beneath me, beating up the night guard who patrolled the back of the house under our bedroom window. I quickly pushed the alarm button to alert our security system. Fortunately, a full detachment of guards soon arrived, but all too late to prevent the dismantling of Mr Singh's burglar-proof gate. They fired several shots into the air to terrify us. It did. They entered our living room and quickly did away with yet another TV set, a state-of-the-art HiFi music system and all of my precious booze, including vintage Jamaican Appleton Estate rum—that hurt. They fled on arrival of the guard company back-up and the local police. We walked around to see our front gate guard tied up to a tree in the bamboo grove. Fortunately he was well enough to smile in relief as we set him free. Our back yard guard, Benjamin, was not so lucky. We found him suffering from severe facial wounds, a broken jaw and skull lacerations. I quickly got Benjamin into my car and sped down to the nearest acceptable hospital—the MP Shah. They rendered expert first aid measures and admitted him to a comfortable semi-private room which I gladly paid for.

On my return home I heard the chilling details of other activities of those beasts. Our twins, Carl and Judy, were visiting at that time and they slept in adjoining bedrooms downstairs. Carl awoke to the sound of gun fire and quickly went next door to his sister's room, grabbed her, and pulled her right up against the wall under the window. He heard the beasts look through the window, fire random shots over their heads, then shout "*hakuna mtu*" (no one here) and move on in their drunken rampage. That brilliant tactical move by Carl certainly saved their lives. The next morning we proceeded to the police station to make our usual lengthy statements taken down in long hand. Mr Singh returned quickly and boarded up the vulnerable areas of the house while he re-did the metal gates.

During these seemingly continuous periods of adversity I tried desperately to keep myself from going crazy. I was deeply disappointed at the path we had to take to maintain our livelihood, security and family cohesion after so many wonderful years in our adopted country. I looked back on the support systems that I had developed over the years with mostly successful outcomes. These included:

My Christian faith. I returned to the values of my parents. I started to go to church again, to St Mark's, a small Anglican church in Westlands near my home. The service was at 7:30 am on Sundays. A small devoted group of worshippers bonded together as we had a true awakening to the promise of our Lord: "I will never leave you or forsake you." I have a crudely painted sign of this by my bedside to this day.

My tennis. For many years I returned to my love of tennis and practised, read books, watched many TV championship finals. After a few years I became fairly good at the game and joined three clubs, which provided me with year-round daily tennis games. First, I joined Invergara, a small club with four courts, a veranda and a small bar. The regulars were mostly African UN and embassy folks and we had good fun and played some fairly accomplished tennis. The next was a multi-racial large sports club called Parklands. It was mostly run by Indians, as Parklands was in the centre of an Indian residential district but whites and newly rich Africans quickly joined also. This club was close to my home so I let it be known that my last patient of the day would be booked so I could get to Parklands, change and be on court for my 5 pm game. I had a number of interesting partners including a Russian spy who played power tennis and was irritated by my weak but well-placed service returns, and an Israeli Mossad agent, formerly an air force fighter pilot instructor who was great fun, especially at the after-game drinks. My most constant and enjoyable partner was an Indian woman who played very good tennis. She maintained a strange aloofness, sending me the message "I am here for tennis only".

For many years I had an ongoing tennis game with Bill Sutherland. He was a black/brown American age mate who had had a checkered career. He had been a conscientious objector during the Vietnam war for which he spent some time in a US prison. He was a devout pacifist and an ardent supporter of the emerging African independence movements. He was in contact with the

African National Congress (ANC) and Nelson Mandela. We became good friends and he made my home his base on his frequent trips from the US to Africa. He was an avid tennis player so you can only imagine our elation when Arthur Ashe and Althea Gibson came into the world of international tennis. Once I picked up Bill at the airport and while driving home I asked him how the struggle (*la luta*) was going. He rambled on about the gains the group made against Portugal in Mozambique (Frelimo) and Angola and the successful blowing up of a weapons train in South Africa by the ANC. At the next stop light, he asked "Can we have a game of tennis?" I turned into Parklands club and enjoyed a couple hours of tennis before nightfall. At home, after showers and one of Margaret's great meals, Bill would invariably ask "What's going on?" meaning "where is the party?"

I chauffeured Bill around quite a bit but I was never able to keep up with his insatiable womanizing. He had been married to a Ghanaian lady and they had several children. Their marriage dissolved and Bill did not seem to play any part in the upbringing of his children. This was upsetting to me and to Margaret but we did not bring it up as a point of difference in our relationship. It was surprising, therefore, when Bill told me one morning that he wanted to speak to me and my daughter Patricia. We went into a room and Bill began his diatribe against Patricia. He accused her of racist behaviour towards our house staff. Pat had an ongoing joking and shouting, "fooling around" relationship with our staff. They accepted this as a sign of love and respect in that sort of way. Bill had his own interpretation and accused her of being a racist and warned her to change her ways. Pat was devastated. She had spent her life identifying as a black woman, marrying a black man, training African youth to be top models and in every way attempting to assist all our African staff, especially those who had a close relationship with her daughter Chris.

Pat broke into tears and left the room while Bill continued his accusations. I told Bill in strong words that he had no right to attack my daughter in that way and I insisted that he apologize. He was surprised that I took such a hard line but I stuck to it and told him that he was no longer welcome in my home. He wrote me a series of letters explaining his views and urging me to "deal with Patricia".

"Fuck you," I said. "You will not come between me and my beloved daughter, get out of my arse.

I never heard from him again. His daughter phoned me to tell me of his demise a few years later. After so many years of fun I was sorry that we had to come to such an acrimonious parting but the word was—don't treat my family like that.

Bill Sutherland with Bishop Tutu.

My running. Yet another stress control method I nurtured was running. After my 50th birthday I took time to review my life. With the medical indices I could summon, I realized that if I continued going in the direction I was currently heading, my life expectancy would be severely shortened. I had already succumbed to these morbid thoughts earlier. At about forty-five years of age. I came to the conclusion that I was pursuing a lifestyle that, with luck, would allow me to live till 65 years of age, at the most. I consulted my life insurance guru and bought a term life policy. This would present my estate with two million dollars if I died before age 65. The premium was reasonable and I faithfully contributed. In a way, I saw that as a licence to continue my raucous life with the assurance that my family would be well looked after when I croaked. At age 60 I seemed to be still alive and relatively healthy despite my being 50 pounds overweight, smoking (and inhaling) pipefuls of tobacco (Sweet Nut), and drinking enormous amounts of Jamaican rum—half a bottle a night. At my epiphany, I realized that this was not the kind of life I really wanted to lead. I then took on the "great escape" program. With great difficulty I did the following: I gave up smoking. This was with the help of my granddaughter Chris, who said that she did not like to see smoke pouring out of my nostrils nor to smell me reeking of tobacco.

"It's smoking or me," she warned.

Punkie was a vital part of my life so I decided that the pipe had to go, and with great difficulty, it did. I started a system of personal fitness, which included a quasi-yoga exercise called "salute to the sun". These stretches ended in a series of push-ups, which were difficult to do at first, but I found myself doing them more and more. I then decided to do one push-up per year of life. When I reached 70 years of age, I did my allotted push-ups then looked up in the direction of the sun and said "Lordy-lord, ain't that enough?"

My back problems forced me to discontinue these wonderful life-saving exercises. To this day I do an altered version of them and I do think they help me a lot. I continued my running. After my daily tennis at Parklands I would run 5 kilometres along the measured track. Sometimes I would do 10. I found that in doing this I increased my lung function and I lost 50 pounds easily without dieting.

I sincerely believe that these measures were the major factors allowing me to be alive today at age 85. All of the adversities that had beset us had taken their toll on our daily lives.

Chapter Twenty-four

FINAL AFRICAN EXIT

Our daughters Judy and Patricia came back to Nairobi and convinced us that we could no longer live in Kenya. Our security was threatened. My professional life was being upset. Our family was separated—overall a gloomy picture, seemingly about to get worse.

"Where shall we go?" I asked, hoping that they would advise me to relocate to the Kenya coast.

"Canada," they insisted.

"But we don't know anything about life in Canada. How shall we survive in that fast-moving society with such cold winters?" I said.

They assured us that it would be possible for us to relocate. We could sell all our properties in Kenya. Patricia and Judy offered to go to Canada to find a place for us to live. I laid out three conditions for such an area.

no overt racial prejudice

a fairly safe environment with minimal crime and insecurity

the least possible cold Canadian winter

Having made this decision in principle, I set about the arduous task of clearing up our Kenyan lives. Doing so included several things:

MY PRACTICE

After my distressing break-up with Cecil Manley, I quickly went to practise in a newly opened doctors' plaza in the MP Shah Hospital. I was warmly welcomed and given a delightful office with ample space and a good line of patient flow. My trusted helper, Margaret, came to open the office with me as did my ever-helpful office manager Sila Shah. Many of my patients followed me there and before long I had built up a substantial practice again. I sought help from young pediatricians and we ran through a number of part-timers moonlighting from the university.

One of these was a young Muslim named Abdul Kareem. He had recently returned from a period of post-graduate training in a prestigious institution in California. His primary goal was to pursue an academic career but he had a family with small children and desperately needed to augment his university salary. He worked well with me and I tried to reward him adequately. I was introduced to his family who were grateful to me for the good fortune I brought to them. I tried to devise ways of transferring my practice. I knew that the Canadian system allowed doctors to sell their private practice. I could not decide on this process. After awhile I realized that Dr Kareem was serving my patients well so one day I told him that I wanted to hand over my practice to him for no payment. He was overcome with disbelief. He told me that his wife and he had been praying to Allah for a way out of their financial and professional predicament. My offer was seen as an answer to this prayer. I proudly embraced him and gladly and gradually handed my practice over to him.

My staff stuck with him and continue to do that to the present. I had hired an office clerk named Maureen. She was a well-educated young African woman, a devout Christian, and she was most helpful in rebuilding my practice. One day she told me that my office needed some refurbishing from the dreary white walls and hanging certificates. She told me that her brother was an artist and would offer his services that weekend. On the following Monday I went to my office to be greeted by excited, giggling staff who pseudo-ceremoniously let me in. Then they showed me an amazing transformation of my room with walls covered by Disney characters and other bright, amusing paintings. I offered payment but it was refused as Maureen explained that the work was done out of love. That kind of amazing affection, devotion, kindness and support did much to rebuild my respect for my African brothers and sisters after such unpleasant experiences elsewhere.

OUR KITISURU HOME

The next great hurdle to be overcome was disposing of our family home. We bought it in 1977 for 120,000

Kenya shillings with a loan from a life insurance company headed by a Canadian friend, Gilles Bissaillon, whose family I had cared for. He readily granted me a mortgage and I got a lawyer friend to do the transfer, an English woman married to a prominent Luo businessman. They lived near to us on Kitisuru Road. She asked to see the property, and I proudly showed her my new purchase. She despondently explained that if I insisted, she would go ahead with the transfer, but I was paying far too much for it. I was shocked, but I insisted that she complete the purchase quickly. Her husband at that time was acquiring a number of properties in desirable areas at bargain prices so I strongly suspected that he himself was eager to purchase mine.

We rented back the property at a nominal rent to the family who sold it to us—a German couple named Wozack. They had recently lost one of their children, a teenage girl, on yet another Mombasa road crash. I did my best to support them by not forcing them to move in the middle of this tragedy. Eventually they moved out of our house to a rented house just up the road. Heinz took his loss very hard and tried to deal with it by substantially increasing his alcohol intake. The Wozacks invited us to their new home after we had moved. It was one of those cool Nairobi nights in mid August so we gathered around the fireplace while Mrs Wozack presented us with delicious finger food in anticipation of her real German *nachtessen*. In the meantime Heinz saw it his duty to ply me with fine brandy, not in the bottom-swirling amount of a brandy snifter but halfway up the giant glass. After I made a few futile attempts to stop Heinz's brandy onslaught, the drink got a hold of me. Soon, slurred speech and double vision overcame me and I excused myself. Against all protest, I grabbed Margaret's arm and pleaded with her to lead me stumbling back home.

We enjoyed our home, which was essentially a country cottage, but soon it became evident that with our ever-returning children and their friends, and an always welcome group of friends passing through on their African safaris, we would have to expand our house. This decision was finalized when Patricia returned with her baby Chris to live with us. We then decided to do some minor extensions. Our friend Don Coombs had just completed a similar construction job and he strongly recommended his friend, an Italian contractor called Sergio. He came, looked around, discussed the changes and gave us an estimate of 300,000 Kenya shillings for the three-month job. I gladly agreed and we braced ourselves for a life that would be disrupted by noise, dirt and many changes of plans. Sergio was a shouting, screaming, cursing man who had little patience with African workers. He was hypertensive, did not comply with his medicines, and after awhile he informed me that he could no longer continue with my job. He said that I owed him a considerable amount of money—about two and a half million shillings, and told me that he would accept one of my recently sub-divided plots of land at the coast as settlement. I was glad to get rid of him and willingly accepted the arrangement. Unfortunately, Sergio died of a massive stroke shortly after.

My daughter Patricia then took over managing the rest of the construction of the wing, which was to become her home. She did an excellent job and the workers were happy to be rid of their hard taskmaster.

When the time came, I was proud to offer my beautiful expanded and refurbished home on the market, convinced that it would fetch a handsome price. One of the first to show interest in it was a rich Indian businessman from a wealthy family whose children I had cared for. Mr Patel walked over the property, examined the house and assured me that it was exactly what he needed for his family. I proposed three million Kenya shillings and he quickly accepted that offer. I asked him to come inside so we could draw up a rough contract that we both would sign. He drew himself up to his full corpulent height and said "Doctor, we Patels are men of our word. Our deal is sealed by a handshake and not on a little piece of paper." He grabbed my hand and we shook on this deal.

I then quickly and securely went ahead with all my plans to leave Kenya. In the meantime, we had also decided that instead of returning to Canada, we would go to Jamaica, buy suitable property and settle down in my homeland. I went to Jamaica, and my sister and her husband Dave showed me a piece of property being sold by a wealthy American that was going at a reasonable price. It was unbelievably beautiful, on a hill overlooking Ocho Rios port, with 25 acres of lush tropical forest and fruit trees—a lovely house with swimming pool and many out-houses. I quickly bought it, expecting to pay with the proceeds of my Kitisuru house sale. On my return I contacted Mr Patel to find out the progress on his purchase of our house. He came to see me and explained that he had shown the house to members of his family and his mother was not pleased with it, for many petty reasons, so he could not buy it. I explained that he had already bought it, as assured by his self-proffered handshake. That meant nothing to him, so he left me high and dry! I learned from this incident never to trust a handshake to complete an agreed business.

I started all over again to sell our Kenyan properties. Fortunately we still had our cottages at the coast, being managed by our 50/50 partners, the Danish couple Finn and Clara. After awhile, we realized that this business, rather than augmenting our income was draining us financially. When we went down to the coast we would be offered a variety of cottages, not all to our own wishes. Clara was the undisputable boss and when we asked to examine the books, we were presented with a variety of figures that made no sense to us. Eventually we decided to split the business into two—we taking six cottages and they taking six. They grabbed the most desirable ones—on the seafront except for one that we insisted on keeping—a beautiful cottage on a cliff overlooking the sea. It had been the favourite of a wealthy Italian who came to stay there regularly.

At this time, my son Carl had returned to live in Kenya and he soon became friendly with an attractive English woman, Shelly. She had been a supervisor in casinos on cruise ships and quickly got employed by the Mombasa Casino. Carl and Shelly moved into the beautiful cottage and did some major refurbishments to make it into a most attractive place to live. We made it our coastal holiday home too. After a few miscarriages, Shelly delivered a lovely little girl. They named her Sylvia

Celeste Forbes. Carl and Shelly continued to manage our cottages well despite constant interference from Clara. Finn had died suddenly one New Year's Day.

We then decided to sell the coastal properties also. Carl embarked on this task. One of the first prospective purchasers was a young businessman named Julian Southern whose mother was a prominent family practitioner. The family had for years spent their Christmas holidays in one of our cottages, on the border with the adjoining property, owned by an entrepreneurial Italian. He convinced us to board up one of our bedroom windows because it overlooked a courtyard where his wealthy guests liked to sunbathe au naturel! We later read in a *Hello* magazine that Brad Pitt and Angelina Jolie had spent their honeymoon there. Julian told me that his family's definition of a heavenly holiday was Christmas at our cottage. We agreed, verbally, on a sale price and left the legal details up to a prominent lawyer. Suffice it to say, three years later I still had not been paid, despite the family having taken virtual possession of our cottage. When the payment did come, it was considerably less than our agreed price and Julian explained that I had made a mistake. I was so pissed off that I accepted the lesser payment just to get these untrustworthy people out of my arse.

Sylvia continued to grow up at the coast with the help of a kind Swahili woman called Amina. She cared for Sylvia lovingly while both Shelly and Carl were away at work. Meanwhile in Nairobi, I was desperately trying to sell my Kitisuru home in order for us to leave Kenya. A variety of folk traipsed through the house, mostly Indians, looking to beat me down on my price. One afternoon I was showing a wealthy Indian my newly refurbished home, especially my shrewdly designed sit-down shower. He gruffly dismissed my boastful explanation with a wave of his hand saying "Don't worry, Doc, I would buy this for the land and would tear down this old house." He didn't buy it! At last a Sikh family approached us and the man immediately contacted his brother in Australia about the offer. Soon the brother arrived, inspected my property and agreed to buy it. I quickly got all my papers together with the help of my lawyer friend, Kirti Shah, and soon the deal was sealed and appropriate payment made. At last, we were able to make concrete plans for us to leave Kenya.

We had made a failed attempt to return to Jamaica, so now we were on our way back to Canada. Pat and Judy had gone to look, starting with Winnipeg. We could not afford any property that was west of Winnipeg, they explained. They landed up in Newfoundland, visiting a variety of family and friends that had all offered "If you ever come back to Canada, please let us know!" Finally we settled on London, a small city in southwestern Ontario. The girls assured us that it met all three conditions of my Wish List and thought that we would live comfortably there.

With much trepidation, Margaret and I decided to make this big move. It was not easy. Fortunately, Patricia took control and arranged all the necessary details— travel plans, the packing and transport of our household effects, the absolutely necessary goodbyes and the financial details. Having arranged for all this, at last we had a departure date, tickets, transport of our belongings and so forth.

About one week before we were due to leave, I was at work at MP Shah Hospital and Patricia was driving to pick me up. She had to pass a primary school just at the time when the kids were going home. They dashed across the road, and on passing the lined up traffic outside the school, one child slammed his hand on Pat's car, ordering her to get out of his way. Pat did not move, but the child complained to a street duty teacher that Patricia's car had hit him. The teacher then came out to Pat to reprimand her. Pat, of course, denied all responsibility for the supposed accident. The teacher then ordered her out of our car and called the police who then ordered her to their station to record a statement. In the meantime, I arrived on the scene and explained the ridiculous accusations that had been laid against my daughter. The police explained that since it related to an alleged assault on a schoolchild it would have to come before a court. They demanded this since Patricia was an expatriate ("a foreigner"). I was to deposit her passport within 24 hours. I knew exactly what this meant so I rushed home and told Patricia to pack up and leave Kenya right away. She understood the severity of this predicament and was on a British Airways plane the next morning to London England.

As Patricia had been our major leaving organizer you can imagine how this left us high and dry. But when we got the phone call from my sister Muffet in London England to tell us that Pat had arrived safely we were greatly relieved. We then decided that the departure date for Marg, Judy and Chris would stand but that I would remain to do the final packing up. They left one night with all their allowable belongings and went to London England then on to London Ontario.

I had a busy time cleaning up our lives in Africa. I had to hand over our Kitisuru home. I would have to decide what to do with all our remaining belongings. Dresses, shoes and other female apparel were distributed among our staff. My beloved army uniforms, panzer boots and regimental paraphernalia were distributed among my night guard, day gatekeepers and other hangers-on. Clearing out one of my drawers, I found a bullet from the .303 rifle I had used on my hunting expeditions. I had wanted to get rid of it for some time as it was illegal to possess unspent cartridges. I tucked it into my jacket and planned to throw it out of the window as I drove to the airport. On clearing my home, I had planned to move into a hotel. My devoted secretary Sila explained that it would be better if I moved into her home with her husband and children for the few days I had left in Kenya. Sila provided me with an apartment within her expansive home. There was ample room to store my remaining belongings and comfortable sleeping quarters. I was amazed at Sila's gracious and efficient hospitality. She did an enormous amount of housework, cooking and preparing her husband and children for their daily activities. The family was strictly vegetarian and I very much enjoyed the meals Sila gave me.

Evenings were spent in frenzied final packing and soon my driver David came to pick me up to go to the airport for the last time. As David drove me I gave him last minute instructions on what to do with my remaining belongings. I also quickly gave him a substantial amount of local currency to distribute among my remaining staff. Unfortunately, I forgot to throw the .303 cartridge out of the window, so on arrival at the airport in the long preliminary examination line I realized that if this deadly weapon was discovered, it would certainly not be possible to leave Kenya that night. I nearly shat my pants, but fortunately I spotted one of the security guards as being in the family of one of my patients. I greeted him warmly.

"Jambo," I shouted. "*Habari mtoto yako?*"("How's your child?"). He recognized me and warmly waved me through. I breathed many sighs of relief and entered the departure lounge, where I spotted a large garbage can and quickly threw the .303 cartridge into it. That was a close shave!

I loaded up with *taka-taka* (rubbish) at the airport gift store. Can't go wrong with Kenyan coffee and *kikois*, the colourful wrap-around worn by coastal folk, male and female. At Heathrow, I searched for John Batkin, my sister Norma's (Muffet's) husband. He was off sailing so his stepdaughter, Anna Kay, picked me up. AK is an extremely attractive, competent woman, partly brought up in our family after the break-up of her parents' marriage. She married a fine young Englishman named Bennett who was a senior advertising executive with a number of large companies, the current being Delta Airlines. AK and Bennett had four children, all boys, and they cared for them with sound, loving guidance and support. Their youngest is now in Oxford University. AK put me up in their lovely cottage and I had the expected let-down reaction. Here I was safe and secure in the company of loving relatives in the beautiful but dark and rainy country. The full effect of my leaving my beloved Africa hit me and I slept and slept. The next morning AK took me back to Heathrow for the final leg of my journey back to Canada.

Chapter Twenty-five

LONDON, ONTARIO

On arrival at Dorval Airport I was surprised. When we left Canada, the government had just completed at enormous expense the new international airport at Mirabel, Quebec—a state-of-the-art facility that occupied what had been an entire village. So finding myself returning to good old Dorval Airport was unexpected. It had been renamed Trudeau International Airport and given a much-needed facelift. I cleared the officious customs and immigration departments, all opening their interrogations in French and seemingly grudgingly switching to English on my humble request. Back in Quebec, I thought. I tried my best to obey the rigid francophone rules while waiting to transfer to my aircraft to Toronto. I found myself succumbing to an all-too-familiar *déjà vu* reaction.

"You're back in white man's country," I reminded myself. "Know your place, do what the man says, don't be uppity and everything will be all right." One of the first habits I reinstated was to call everyone I spoke to "sir" or "ma'am". This habit is so deeply ingrained in me that to this day, I keep it up with all strangers with whom I am in contact whether black or white, young or old. I guess that when I die, and the mortician is preparing me for my pre-cremation viewing, I shall (*sotto voce*) whisper "thank you, sir (or ma'am)".

Patricia met me in Toronto at the Pearson airport. She led me to a lovely big car, a Honda SUV, and began what was to become a regular trip for us—Toronto to London Ontario, on the 401 superhighway, a multilane road with an enormous amount of traffic barrelling down it. It has many rules such as that trucks must not drive in the fast lane which was for overtaking only. "Tail gaiting" was supposed to be forbidden, and exceeding the speed limit could be electronically monitored and the fined payment delivered by mail. Patricia knew all the rules and I was amazed at her efficient, safe driving habits. After an enjoyable two-hour drive we arrived in London Ontario. I was impressed by this medium-sized city of 350,000 which seemed to have all one could ever need including a first-class university, many superb hospitals, good restaurants, lovely housing and good roads.

We arrived at our first Canadian rented apartment, a small place on a street that seemed to have the railway line driving through it. The trains sometimes took 30 minutes to cross by our apartment—precluding sleep and conversation. But the joy of reuniting with my wife and family overcame any apprehension I had about our new home. We quickly set about finding a definitive home. Patricia had contacted a real estate agent, a friendly, trustworthy and experienced man who seemed genuinely interested in us and tried his best to respond to our unique needs. His name was Guy Laflamme and we became good friends. He had already shown Pat and Margaret a number of properties and they all seemed to short-list one in a pleasant area of London called Byron. It was a three-bedroom detached house with adequate facilities, seemingly all we needed, so we quickly agreed to purchase it. We settled in as best we could as our belongings had not arrived in the container from Africa.

We purchased enough furniture to make us comfortable and quickly adjusted to the Canadian life of cooking, washing, cleaning the house and garden, and watching TV. I did notice that our next-door neighbour seemed to be addicted to TV. At that time I began to notice also a number of reports of strange crimes occurring mostly in Toronto and surrounding areas. Criminals included pedophiles, serial killers and strange unsolved murders. I was shocked as the crimes were not what I expected, indeed, they were what we were running away from. Jokingly, I postulated that our aloof unfriendly neighbour was indeed a serial killer and warned my family to beware of him. Soon our container came from Africa, backed into our driveway and unloaded our precious African belongings. When they were all unloaded we realized the terrible truth. We could not fit all our belongings into the house. Grudgingly, we decided to move. Not long after, Patricia presented us with a large house in the same Byron region. It seemed to be all we needed; it had five bedrooms, large grounds, a swimming pool and a pleasant neighborhood. We decided to sell our first home and buy this one. It was a good move, as we all settled in well.

Soon we found a school for Chris and I became completely engrossed in the upkeep of our large garden. Gardening was an unusual role for me as I do not have a green thumb. On the contrary, every plant I handle turns over and dies! One fall, I visited the garden centre and purchased a number of tulip bulbs which I was assured would bloom in the spring! I remember seeing tulips in Holland and I greatly desired a garden wall full of them. So I purchased the lot and digging vigorously, I planted them all. Two weeks later on my usual watering round, I found the squirrels had dug up the entire lot! I said some bad words and swore never to try that kind of gardening again.

My other major occupation was learning to navigate the computer. This meant finding my way around email and looking for things on Google. The effort was a frustrating one, as invariably I would get stuck at some essential time. In despair I would shout for my granddaughter—"Punkie!" I would scream, until she appeared, usually bleary-eyed from sleep or study, to patiently lead me through this electronic morass to some sort of promised e-land.

After awhile, in her kind, loving way she informed me, "Baka, I can't keep running every time you scream at me. You have to learn how to do things yourself on the computer."

I agreed and she gently led me through computer land. This was in contrast to her mother, who would quickly come at my call, order me to move over from the machine, correct my mistakes, hand the mouse back to me and tell me to carry on.

"What did I do wrong?" I would ask. "What should I do next time?"

"Don't worry," she would curtly reply.

That was the beginning of a disturbing relationship I had with Pat. She was aware of the many shortcomings in my attempt to resettle in Canada but was impatient and disappointed with my failures.

I had to re-apply for my driver's licence as my previous one had expired and my age militated against automatic renewal. Patricia tried to teach me how to do Canadian driving. I found this situation embarrassing as I had driven from the age of 16 in many different countries with never an accident, despite serious challenges. Pat encouraged me to take the senior drivers course offered by CARP (Canadian Association of Retired Persons), which we had joined. A professional instructor, Dan Procop, came to my house and gave me a month's intensive senior driver re-education course. I was grateful to him for introducing me to the fine points of Canadian driving that had not been in place when I left 45 years ago. He then felt that I was fit to take the re-exam. I reported to the centre for the written exam which I passed easily.

On the appointed day I returned for my practical road test. Unfortunately, this was the first day of the snow storm season. I was assigned to my examiner, a hung-over Irishman with a clipboard. He ordered me to go onto the highway. I could barely see the road due to the blinding snow. I remembered my driving booklet instructing me to drive according to the posted speed limits but to adjust to prevailing conditions. The posted speed was 70 kilometres per hour but the snow was so blinding that I barely crept along at 30 to 40 kilometres per hour as did the rest of the traffic. I obeyed all the examiner's instructions while he made notes on his clipboard and I returned safely to the test centre. He gruffly handed me a copy of his notes and told me to report to the desk. There I was told that I had failed the test because I drove too slowly and did not obey the posted speed limits. I tried to explain my predicament but was summarily dismissed with a return appointment if I wished to continue. Needless to say, I was pissed off with the way I was treated.

I returned to Dan Procop and told him my story. He was not surprised and explained that many seniors failed at their first road test, more a punishment than an assessment. He gave me a few more lessons and encouraged me to take the test again. Fortunately I passed. I was given a licence that forbade me from driving the 400-series highways unless accompanied by a fully licensed driver and excluding me from driving if I had any detectable alcohol in my breath or blood tests. That put an end to my night partying. Just as well, as I had no friends with whom to enjoy such luxuries.

I still take regular age-related driving tests at which we old geezers are urged to take taxis instead. Fortunately I am enlisted with a reliable taxi company called Checkers that responds quickly to my requests and signs me up for a monthly payment on my VIP taxi card. Patricia also had to put up with many other of my predicaments, not the least of which was finding my car in the parking lot of a supermarket. I would push my shopping cart and view the vast array of parked cars, trying to remember where I left mine. After many futile efforts I would call Pat from my cell phone and she would quickly arrive to lead me to my lost car with the help of a number of electronic devices.

By far the worst re-entry buffeting I experienced was my attempt to re-enter the medical profession. I had always tried desperately to live up to the highest standard of my profession. So when I returned to Canada, the home of my professional training, with my registration in various provincial colleges of medicine, I was sure that I would be welcomed back with open arms—the prodigal son so to speak. After a few months of re-settling, I decided to forgo my aim of retirement and seek re-entry into the mainstream of Canadian medical life. When I left Canada I had contacted the various colleges of medicine with whom I had registered in Ontario, Quebec and Nova Scotia, telling them of my plan to spend my life in the service of patients in Africa and asking for their advice on the process by which I could re-register when I returned to Canada. They all reassured me that they admired my decision to serve in Africa and on my return I would merely have to contact them and they would re-enlist me. I set about to do just this and they all replied that due to my prolonged absence from medical practice in Canada I would have to be re-assessed to establish my fitness to practise here.

This was a royal kick in the ass. I was deeply disappointed but I was determined not to end my professional career (distinguished as I thought it was) on my hands and knees as a mendicant, angry, disappointed old doctor. I duly applied, took the prescribed exams and became re-registered in Ontario as a pediatrician—a great relief for me.

I had even tried to rejoin the Canadian Pediatric Society (CPS). It was founded by my colleagues Elizabeth and Don Hillman and I had had some small part in its inception. I received a terse answer to my request, which said that since I had ticked the "retired" box I was no longer worthy of gaining membership in the CPS—another kick in the balls. I wrote Liz Hillman and she angrily ordered the CPS to re-instate me.

One of my greatest losses was that of my good friends whom I had had throughout the years. Most of my medical friends were either retired, had moved away, were dead, or did not want to reply to my communications. I had to accept this situation grudgingly because they had been good friends, with many of whom like Werner Woelber and Chico Kiteala I had shared good times and family connections.

Our desperate attempts to re-establish friendships in Canada led us back to our military lives. We regained contact with a close friend, Ramsay Withers. On hearing of my return, Ramsay immediately told me about the upcoming regimental reunion of the RCDs in Ottawa. We willingly signed up. Marg and I went to the opening cocktail party. Ramsay and Allison introduced us to RCD friends. Ramsay was always effusive when introducing me, dwelling in great length on my distinguished service in Africa. We had followed Ramsay's career with interest and pride. He served with distinction in the Korean war and was emphatic about his view that this was Canada's forgotten war despite heavy losses. He had been the commander of the Canadian forces in the north for many years, based in Whitehorse. Allison had many interesting and fun-producing tales of their life in the land of the midnight sun. Ramsay achieved the highest rank in the Canadian military—Chief of General Staff, as a full general. He held this post, serving with distinction until his retirement. Ramsay and Ali insisted that we stay with them for the reunion—what an enjoyable time. Ramsay had warned me that the official dinner dance was a formal affair so in lieu of full regimental dress (red coats), I could wear a dinner jacket but with full medals. I explained that I did not have any medals. He protested, explaining that at least I had the NATO service medal from my time in Germany. He quickly arranged this.

Ramsay and Allison lived in a delightful apartment not far from Parliament Hill. We had a warm welcome and a lovely meal prepared fastidiously by General Withers while Allison prepared her world-renowned martinis. The following night, after a day of elaborate regimental affairs we all got dressed up and proceeded to the fancy hotel. The dinner dance was a colourful affair with the soldiers dressed in their most formal dress—red jackets dripping with medals while carrying elaborate riding crops. I was gulping down my champagne when a tall, aging soldier with many medals and sleeves full of stripes came up to me and said "Captain Forbes, do you remember me?" I looked closely and admitted that I did not.

"I was Corporal Urbanowski. I was sent to be your bat man in Iserlohn. When I came to your apartment you explained that I was to iron your uniform and shine your shoes. Ho ho ho! I guess I told you where to get off. Ho ho ho." I had understood that these were the duties of a bat man as explained to me by Captain Simon Bradish-Elems. He was an exchange officer from our mother regiment in England, "The Royals", the distinguished British cavalry regiment. We became good friends as he explained that his duty was not only to serve time with the RCD but to try to teach proper British manners, behaviour and customs. Later I learned that Simon was a distant member of the English royal family, with all the warts that this entailed. I sincerely apologized to Corporal (now Major) Urbanowski and we had several drinks together. We had a wonderful meal and then the dancing. I was proud to be in such exalted company. Margaret and I enjoyed some slow dancing and I even summoned up the courage to ask the general's wife, Allison, to dance. The next day after a late, elaborate breakfast prepared by Ramsay we went to the Canadian War Museum. Ramsay is one of the prominent members of their board and he gave me a tour of this great Canadian facility. My god-daughter Leslie recently phoned to tell me that both Ali and Ramsey had passed away.

On our return to London, Margaret and I were much impressed by all that we had experienced. We were happy to be so kindly received back into Canada after many years in the African bush.

I then took stock of our financial resources. Fortunately we had received payment from the sale of some of our Kenyan properties. This looked good on paper so we went to our bank and asked them to invest this new wealth in such a way that I could retire from work and make some interest on our substantial investment. We were allotted a financial adviser who promised us a good return on our investment. We trustingly handed over our funds to him and awaited monthly good news. The news came but it was not good! Month after month our investment figures were decreasing instead of increasing as we had been promised. We were told that this was 2008 and the whole financial world was collapsing. After a frantic discussion with some friends we were advised to get out of that bank and to invest with a wonderful investment planner who would pull us back from our losses and lead us to the promise land. We gladly grabbed onto John McNeil who outlined a strategy to recover our substantial losses. John was a tall, good-looking man who seemed to know everything about investments. He gladly shared his knowledge with us and we fell for it hook, line and sinker. Our losses seemed to be less and we were presented with plans that involved borrowing significant amounts of money to buy some deals that would provide much valuable return. This was called "margins". Somehow, the monthly reports did not reflect the magic recovery numbers we expected so once again I figured that we were in deep shit. My College of Medicine, to which I pay substantial amounts in fees, advertised that they provide doctors with free financial advice. I saw one of these advisers and provided my monthly reports to him. He took one look at them and barked "Margins? We don't deal with those!" He pushed all the papers back to me, got up and left as if I had presented him with a plan to rob a bank or run a whorehouse. I was up a tree.

Here I was with an increasing amount of capital, which my son Carl sent me on selling off our cottages on the Kenya coast for amounts greater than I had anticipated. So our financial situation was improving dramatically but our losses were formidable. One of my few friends in London was a colleague named Dr Billy de Vries. Billy was a pediatric oncologist, one of Canada's pioneers in the aggressive treatment of children's cancer, especially leukemia and lymphoma. He was a professor at the University of Western Ontario—a great doctor but a poor businessman. After awhile he realized that he was deeply in trouble with the Canadian Revenue Authority over his income tax. In his twisted logic he thought that he could go to Saudi Arabia, make mega tax-free bucks, then come back to Canada and settle all his debts. So he took his wife, Irma, an accomplished artist, to Saudi Arabia where they lived the cloistered life of expatriates, made a lot of money, and prepared to return to Canada. He then learned that the supposed tax-free salary he had made was indeed taxable in Canada so he was again up a tree. He devised a plan to return to Canada via Nairobi where he could make lots of money. He contacted me and I gladly offered him a job in my practice. We became good friends and he worked hard and efficiently. We had many pleasant evenings together and I was most impressed by

Irma's paintings. Unfortunately, all his plans to regain his funds by importing Mercedes Benz cars from Saudi to sell at enormous profits in Kenya failed miserably.

On our planned return to Canada, Pat and Judy came to London Ontario and visited Billy and Irma, who were very hospitable. That is partly how we landed up in this nice town. I often met with Billy and I told him of my financial predicament. He quickly explained his own financial problems and told me about a fine gentleman who managed his funds and eventually turned them around to be profit making. I eagerly met this man—Harry Thiel, a senior, honest, deeply religious Catholic (like Billy). He explained that he was going away to the Camino but my account would be looked after by his son Milton. From then on our funds have been managed in a concerned, efficient way and I think that Marg and I will be able to survive in financial security—*enshallah*. That whole financial fiasco affected me a great deal and I had many sleepless nights worrying about our eventual outcome. I had seen old men like me welcoming shoppers to Walmart, clearing off sidewalks, wrapping groceries at supermarkets, and so forth, and I thanked God that I did not have to do this now, and prayed that I would never have to.

Soon it became evident that our big house in Byron was too large for us. Patricia had been our mainstay with her support and guidance. She was actively pursuing her profession as a ballroom dancing instructor. She quickly established her own business, a franchise. Her classes were much in demand. After awhile her manager became unhappy with her requests and she decided to break her contact with him. This involved some legal fees which we were able to manage. She then started her own dance instruction studio and called it Passion for Dance, which she pursues to this day. Pat is a beautiful woman; she once modeled for *Vogue* magazine so inevitably, she attracted a number of men hopeful to gain her favours. She always maintained a degree of aloofness to prospective suitors. A few did break through this barrier but did not last long.

Then came Mr Right—James. He was an older gentleman from the UK who was one of her dance students. He came with a lot of baggage—a failed marriage and two accidentally conceived children who were now in their teens. Nevertheless, she was very attentive to him and he was often in our home. In fact I became friends with Mr Right. By this time we had acquired a dog, a lovely white puppy that we named Teddy. He was a malti-poo and he endeared himself to us. I am not a dog lover but I enjoyed this little critter and chased him around the house day and night. Pat then became very serious with James, who lived in Toronto. Soon she started to make regular trips to Toronto to see him on various excuses—moving house, tidying up his home, assisting in his business, and so forth. These trips entailed leaving Teddy at home with us. That meant that Teddy would sleep in our bed between Margaret and me! After awhile I became accustomed to this but I really hated having to share my bed with a dog. Nevertheless Pat's devotion to James continued, and so did our babysitting duties with Teddy. Then abruptly, Pat's relationship with James ended. He committed the unpardonable sin of forgetting an important anniversary. I was pleased to see this development as this self-centred old man was not, in my mind, worthy of the love and support that my daughter provided him.

At that time Chris was finishing her high school. She also attracted a variety of young men. Initially, they were invariably black men. One of them she met in Toronto during an abortive York University term—the university was closed three months after she started due to a faculty strike. This young man came to London one weekend to visit her. He wore the popular black youth uniform and appeared at our dining table for my carefully prepared meal wearing a cap perched over one ear, a ragged jean vest, a baggy, long-crotched pair of trousers and expensive athletic shoes. He offhandedly shook my hand and then started to refuse the food I had offered him. At the end I dished out his ice cream which he shoved away grunting "ice cream is gross". I asked Chris what that meant but she was too embarrassed to answer. A long-lasting relationship with a young black student from Kenya also ended on protestations from his parents. They were concerned that their son was getting too deeply involved with a woman who was not from the proper Kenyan tribe. After awhile Chris moved out of our house to live closer to her school. By now, she was a student at Fanshawe College, the foremost community college in London. She shared an apartment with a good friend, a young white man. They both assured me that their relationship was purely platonic. Chris did well at school, taking media studies but she later switched to psychology.

All these changes had a domino effect on our lives. Pat decided that the five-bedroom house we occupied was far too big for the three of us. We discussed a number of options. Finally, we decided to jointly finance the purchase of a condo for Pat; Chris, Margaret and I would move into a retirement home. We set about to sell our beautiful home in a most desirable area of London. Our trusted estate agent went about this onerous job, dealing with a number of wheelers and dealers trying to beat down our asking price. To me, Guy seemed too gentlemanly to handle these scoundrels as I was desperately trying to obtain the maximum amount possible in order to secure our retirement nest egg, so we terminated his agency and Pat and I tried to sell the property ourselves. After many months with no serious buyers and a deluge of con men, I mentioned my predicament to a friend from my church. He told me that he had a relative who was a superb house salesman who could help us and we met with him. He was a friendly, mature gentleman who was full of corny jokes. He promised to sell the house within three months if we would allow him to set the final price. Grudgingly, we agreed and in about two months we had a firm buyer at a price less than my expectation but we carried through. I had examined a number of retirement homes and decided on one that I hoped would be suitable—Woods Hills, an old nunnery and later a girls' college. It is an imposing building on a mountain overlooking the middle of the city. It had just been taken over by an international retirement home business. We were allotted a two-bedroom apartment in the self-service division of the home next to the assisted living wing. With great difficulty, we moved our essential belongings to our fourth-floor apartment and tried to settle in. Shortly, we found this apartment too small for us and our now inseparable belongings.

We had just settled in when a series of mishaps occurred. Margaret fell in the shower and we had great difficulty getting her up. Then she had an unexplained dizzy spell and fell in the living room. I could not get her up so I called the front desk for help. The home director, a tall lady, quickly came with the on-duty concierge. They gave Margaret stern instructions on how to get up and with their help, she took to her bed.

I was most grateful to them for their assistance. But the next day we had a phone call from the director, who ordered us to her office. I was away, so Patricia went and was given a lecture on the proper way to deal with such emergencies. The director explained that it was not their duty to look after apartment residents and if we needed help, we should call 911. This pissed me off and I set up a system that would always leave Margaret protected or supervised. Shortly later, I was told that a more suitable apartment was now available on the fifth floor so we quickly grabbed it up—yet another move that Pat and Chris organized. Our new apartment was much larger and more comfortable. The only problem was that my long-awaited "room with a view" was replaced by an expansive view of the garbage depot and collection area—can't have everything!

By that time I was involved in my new project—providing health care to an Indian reserve on Walpole Island. I had developed a close friendship with a man named Paul Blanchard, who was super energetic, intelligent and ambitious. He had roots in East Africa and indeed had adopted children from Uganda and Haiti. He asked me to accompany him to the opening of a pharmacy in the Walpole Island Indian reserve, which was on a river just across from Michigan and not far from Detroit. About 5000 Indians lived on this island. It was a non-seeded territory and a doctor had never practised there. A kind-hearted, wealthy, Jewish pharmacist from Toronto named David Garsovitz had given a substantial gift to the reserve to build a pharmacy, which would create income for the community. Paul drove me down for the grand opening of this imposing building. Paul knew the community well because he had built a police station there the previous year. I listened with admiration to all the speeches and plans that the chief outlined for developing health services on the island.

Paul then introduced me to the chief, Joey Gilbert, an imposing, humble and sincere gentleman. Paul introduced me as "Dr Colin Forbes".

"A real doctor?" the chief asked.

"Yes," I said. "I am a pediatrician."

He grabbed me by the arm, looked me in the eye and pleaded "Help us, doc!".

"I will, chief," I replied.

We then walked around to the back of the pharmacy and quickly outlined the plans for a clinic. Paul ordered a full construction plan to be drawn up and three months later, I opened the Walpole Island Medical Clinic. I was given a nurse-manager-receptionist, Leona Isaacs. She was an experienced Indian woman, eager to get things going. We planned the entire operation of the clinic—the reception, waiting room, doctor's office, bookings for return appointments, prescriptions from the pharmacy and special instructions. It all went wonderfully well. The patients were at first wary of the entire operation, suspicious that it would be yet another trick played on the reserve by the various levels of government. At first, our attendees were few so I took advantage of this time to organize and re-organize our operation with Leona's advice and guidance. It was always welcoming for me to hear her frank advice, such as "We Indians don't do things that way", "That won't work, try it our way", and so forth.

I left London at 9 am on Monday mornings and drove two hours to Walpole Island along country roads, sometimes covered by fog but with an abundance of farm tractors and school buses. I would book into the Oaks Hotel in Wallaceburg then proceed over the causeway to my clinic. I explained at the onset that I would work all day through but due to my old African habits I would have to break for one hour for a rest, not a lunch. This worked well and by 5 pm I would quit.

Nights were long in the Oaks Hotel so after a boring supper I would take my glass of Merlot wine to my room and start to write my play—a documentation of my days as a sleeping car porter on the CPR while I was a pre-med student at McGill. The play just flowed out and in three months I had completed *All Aboard*. It was produced at the Palace Theatre in London for a one-week run in September 2013. It gained positive reviews and I am now pursuing the possibility of making it into a movie.

Wednesday was difficult as I would check out of the Oaks, report early to work, then go right through till

I saw the last patient at around 1 pm. I then set off on the road back to London, having had to forgo my usual afternoon sleep. It was inevitable that the drive would involve me in some near-miss sleep disasters. I learned that my car radio had stations that seemed to provide music from different speakers in my car. I searched for such stations on my way back, and turned the volume up high in an attempt to keep awake. I rejoiced when I saw the road sign to Lambeth, a village near London, and my increased heart rate warned me that I was near home.

On reaching home, I realized that my absences were having their effect on Margaret. She was anxious, fearful for my safety and at times seemed disoriented. I shared these concerns with Pat, Chris and Judy and they all concurred with my observations. We decided to elicit the help of our family doctor, Dr Sunderji. He listened to our concerns about Margaret's many health problems: her diagnosed atrial fibrilation, her increasing joint pains in her knees, shoulder and groin. The doctor made the appropriate consultations and soon we were on the diagnostic road. The most important was an assessment at the state-of-the-art geriatric centre at Parkwood Hospital. There we met with a number of experts, geriatric nursing specialists and psychologists. This all took about three hours and a final report was presented to the head of the unit, Dr Kane. This kind, brilliant professional woman reviewed all the tests and informed us that the final diagnosis for Margaret's condition was early dementia. She explained that dementia is a spectrum, often leading to Alzheimer's disease. She outlined a full program of support and direction that could help to delay Margaret's disease progression. This news was shocking to us but we determined to follow the program Dr Kane outlined. She gave us an appointment for a follow-up in one year's time—late November of 2014.

We then had to make decisions about our future. We had settled in Woods Hills and that seemed to be satisfactory but I explained that I had an overwhelming anxiety brought on by the Canadian winter. I impulsively decided that we should escape to Jamaica for three months—from mid-December to the end of March. We scoured the internet and found that air miles collected from one of our bank accounts would allow Margaret and me to fly to Montego Bay and return in the low season in business class.

Chapter Twenty-six

JAMAICAN WINTER HOLIDAY

We quickly set up the trip and in due course we were on our way to Montego Bay—a mere four-hour flight. We had requested assisted boarding which meant being taken through all the various boarding procedures in wheel chairs expertly guided by staff. In the aircraft, we were provided with adequate meals and an abundance of bubbly. Before we left I had to finalize our financial responsibilities for the period that we were away.

On arrival in Montego Bay we anxiously sought our family. For a long time I could not find any of them. After about half an hour looking at Jamaican faces I eventually saw my brother-in-law, Dave, the Guyanese husband of my sister Fay. He was surprised that we had not seen him before and he quickly led us to the restaurant where Fay was patiently waiting. After a warm reunion, we boarded their car, a comfortable SUV driven by Fay. I was surprised at this but relieved at the expert quality of her driving. It is a two-hour drive along the beautiful winding north coast road to Ocho Rios. We were overwhelmed by this beauty and impressed by Fay's deft manoeuvring through these twisting roads. We arrived at Pilgrim's Lodge, our new home, reached by climbing up a steep mountain road called Fern Gully—one of the most dramatic roads in the world. From the coastal region of Ocho Rios it rises sharply up a steep hill with endless sharp corners, each approached with large blasts of the horn. In former days, the road was covered by giant ferns, like the nave of a cathedral, making it dark enough to require car lights. Unfortunately, due to the exhaust fumes from large trucks (now banned), the ferns have been virtually wiped out with only a few small ones remaining.

At the top of the road a welcome sign proclaimed a tourist trap run by an entrepreneuring Rastafarian affectionately called Colonel and his family. We turned right at Colonel's and stopped at his emporium to view his local products. My nephew Roger, my late brother Ralph's son, often visits Colonel to enjoy a game of the local Jamaican male pastime, dominos, washed down by white "overproof" rum. Pilgrim's Lodge is a centuries-old Jamaican Great House. Dave and Fay bought it from a wealthy American who had restored much of it. They were then living in Washington DC where Dave had worked with the World Bank as an agronomist, mostly on sugar, for many years. On his retirement, Dave and Fay decided to move to Pilgrim's Lodge to set up their home. It was an idyllic setting with a large surrounding farm and it quickly became a lodestone to the entire Forbes and Douglas families and their friends or friends' friends. Successive cohorts sat for the proscribed photo on the front steps. Fay and Dave were gracious, caring hosts and these visits invariably included sumptuous Jamaican meals.

Jamaican culture is centuries old, steeped in plantation lore, slavery and subsequent emancipation. Rum, sugar, bananas and coconuts ruled the economy for many years. Now tourism and the ever-present blaring Jamaican music of Bob Marley rule. OK, Rastafarian culture is also evident. Rastas are self-appointed members of a modern-day religion. Its roots are in the hills overlooking Kingston. Many disgruntled ex-service men, unable to gain the rewards given to white and brown officer class veterans of the Second World War, set up these virtual communes. They decided to establish their own way of life. They worshipped His Excellency Haile Selassie of Ethiopia and proclaimed him as the incarnation of God. They let their hair grow in its natural course without cutting and they smoked marijuana which they called the weed of life. Usually they were a peaceful group, earning their living by making things such as hammocks and rubber tyre sandals, which they sold by the roadside. They have a strict life code—nutritionally no salt, pork or alcohol. Rastafarianism is now an international religion and members continue their quest towards peace in their own way. They have a language of their own, referring to themselves as "I and I" or proclaiming "*irie*" (everything is all right), and so forth. Colonel is a Rasta and he became a good friend of mine, especially when I told him that I was a friend of Dr Johannes Workneh Martin who was the personal physician to His Excellency Haile Selassie. I explained that Johnny Martin had introduced me to Haile. Colonel was most impressed.

We quickly settled into Pilgrim's Lodge and enjoyed every aspect of our life there. It was such a joy to awaken to the 6 am sunrise and look out of the window to see a huge cruise ship entering Ocho Rios harbour. Later that evening, we would see it leaving with lights blazing in the Caribbean. Margaret had a difficult time settling in. Her memory processes were confusing so I had to repeatedly explain our various family members: "Roger is my late brother's son, Chloe is his wife, Brent and Billy are their children." We also met Janice, Ralph's first child. She was now a senior executive with a renowned hotel empire. She has a home on a plot near Pilgrim's Lodge, with beautiful architecture and design and finished with excellent detail by Roger. We settled into the rather rigid routines of Dave and Fay: breakfast: a new menu every day and then a post-prandial rant by Fay on the state of the Jamaican nation—hopeless, crooked, insoluble. This took us into mid-day when Marg and I settled in for our nap. In the afternoon we had our main meal, a masterpiece created by Fay and her trusty helper Cindy. Much of it was gleaned from their closely watched Food Channel downstairs on television. Despite this close bond between Fay and Cindy, there remained episodes of friction between them which disturbed me. Cindy was often reprimanded loudly by Fay for some often-minimal mistake or omission. Nevertheless, Cindy seemed to brush it off, and when I questioned her she smiled, shrugged and said "That's Miss Fay". Despite these outbursts Fay remains very close to Cindy. She continues to support her in her every family need (Cindy has seven children) and she always donates substantial sums of money to Cindy's family and to many other families in the area. Margaret slept a lot but after awhile she began to take part in the many family affairs.

Fay had one of her famous Pilgrim's Lodge Christmas dinners. There were 25 people at the enormous table. After a lengthy grace (which accompanied all our meals) we dug into a memorable feast of Jamaican food. The standard ham, turkey and beef were augmented by salt fish and ackee, a local exotic vegetable, breadfruit, avocado, plantain, rice and peas, bammie (cassava cake) and so forth. What a glorious feast! It was also a great opportunity for me to touch base with my extended family from Kingston—my cousins Audrey and Rosie, and a newfound cousin, Ann Marie. Nights were spent downstairs in front of the television, on which only specific stations were available. First the local news, then a snippet of the BBC and then a sports channel which showed the latest international tennis. Dave had been an expert tennis player and with my former experiences as an enthusiastic player we had good times shouting and screaming at the line calls. Interspersed were track and field events, inevitably featuring the Jamaican hero Usain Bolt winning his marvelous races.

Fay and Dave have a large group of friends so there was an abundance of dinners and parties to attend. Some of these included a trip to a local jerk house at nearby

Walker's Wood, a small village that has a factory producing the highly regarded jerk. Jerk is a Jamaican sauce applied to various meats and fish. It is made on a barbeque fired by wood from the pimento tree, indigenous to Jamaica. It is highly spiced and makes a very enjoyable meal if you can tolerate the pepper.

The Jamaican language is indeed a unique brand of English. It is said that it is derived from medieval English interspersed with African words and expressions and flavoured with residual Spanish. I was surprised to find that it had not only survived the many years that I had been away but indeed it has become the bonding lingua franca of the majority of Jamaicans, primarily black people. They spoke it exclusively among themselves and only made seemingly painful efforts to clean up their speech with employers and visitors. Cindy spoke this patois in a flowery, rapid way. I understood very little of what she said. I was ashamed of this and made feeble excuses about being away for such a long time. Fay translated for her and many of the other helpers, continuously reprimanding them for not speaking proper English—fat chance. For many years, Dave took it upon himself to wage a war against the bastardization of the English language by Jamaicans. He told stories of Jamaicans applying for much-needed jobs and being refused because the prospective employers could not understand them—thereby driving young Jamaicans into a life of crime. I remembered my own childhood and my mother's discomfort when I broke out into patois. "You will not speak like that here," she would insist. "We speak English in this house."

Since the popularity of Jamaican music internationally, especially Bob Marley's brand of singing, the patois has been granted a de facto place of honour, even in the university, where it is taught as a subject. I still love to speak what I remember of it and I often lapse into a long diatribe in patois at my dining table on the current topic of interest. It is unintelligible to the rest of my Canadian family, who write me off as a victim of too much wine. In Jamaica, I did notice a certain amount of discord in the house between Fay and Dave. I often accompanied Dave down Fern Gully, always an exciting experience, to pick up a variety of produce from the list Fay had given him. We went into a number of stores and I insisted in paying the food bill as Marg and I were staying at their home.

The town shopping involved a number of stops to obtain various foods from a variety of people, such as yams from Ruby. Ruby operated a clandestine stall outside the gates of St Anne's market. She is an aged, toothless woman, whom our family had known for many years. My brother-in-law, the Englishman John Batkin, claimed to be in love with her (or so she said) and sent regular gifts from England (clothes for Ruby and her family and dime-store watches that my sister Muffet collected from coupons). Ruby herself had a helper called Matt. He was a feeble-minded gentleman who ran through the market picking up produce ordered by Fay via Ruby. I used to remain in the car at this time and I was so fascinated by this beggar's opera that I invariably gave a modest reward to Matt for his loyal service. Usually when the list was completed, Ruby would appear at my car window and with a quiet compelling voice convince me to part with another substantial amount of Jamaican dollars for some good cause—the burial of a cousin or the payment of a grandson's school fees. How could I refuse? We would then head out of town past Colonel's turn-off to a small village nearby. On our parking the car, a ragged Rastafarian would emerge from the bushes. Dave would then read out the list: irish potatoes, sweet potatoes, sour sop and "nice" pears (avocados). The Rasta would appear, as if by magic, to present all of these foods. Then came the moment of reckoning. Dave would record each purchase and add them up and invariably I would pay for them. We would then stop at Colonel's for our eggs. He would deliver them to me, smilingly reminding me that I was due to visit him to play dominos and drink overproof rum.

These excursions were precious to me, coming from the sterilized, sometimes hostile experiences in Canada. I marvelled at the industry, devotion, honesty and pleasure demonstrated by these wonderful folk—my countrymen and women and now my real friends. I became deeply involved with the day-to-day occurrences of my own family. My nephew Roger was now unemployed and he remained at home looking after his two children while his wife Chloe worked as a manager in a housing complex in Ocho Rios. She once worked in Kingston and drove the hazardous two-and-a-half-hour journey, day and night, for a few years. Chloe is a strong Jamaican brown woman from a deeply religious family in Spanish Town. She is devoted to her husband Roger and their two children, Brent (10 years old) and Billy (2 years old). Brent was admitted to Jamaica's top boarding school, Monroe.

My brother Val left a long teaching career in London England to be headmaster of this prestigious school.

Brent was a highly intelligent lad who was anxious to do well at Monroe. Unfortunately something went wrong, his performance academically and socially deteriorated rapidly, and he was suspended for a short while. We were all upset about this and we had a serious brain-storming session to try to rehabilitate him. Eventually he returned in good standing and is now doing well. Dave and Fay also pointed out to me that Billy did not seem to be progressing well. He had no speech at two years and his motor development was also delayed. Roger was in complete charge of Billy during the day and he often brought him to Fay's place. Billy was very attached to Dave and the two would spend long times together. Dave introduced him to music by singing to him and urging him to play their piano which he did, not with the seemingly meaningless banging of a two-year-old but what seemed to be a meaningful picking away at the notes. I noticed this feat and wondered if it was not a form of autism spectrum disorder. I urged the family to pursue this possibility. They did and I recently received the final report of the developmental specialist who indeed diagnosed Billy as having autism. She also recommended chromosomal studies to look into the possibility of that being responsible for some of the facial dimorphisms which I had also noted.

Despite all these drawbacks, Margaret and I continued to enjoy the idyllic experiences we were having in Jamaica. I encouraged Margaret to walk around the property in the afternoons. That was the time when Dave gave his two dogs their daily exercises, chasing balls and sticks around the garden. We walked around this beautiful ring of colourful flowers and trees. It was most invigorating for both of us, more so for Margaret who deliberately pointed out the mixture of beautiful colours around the lawn. I was proud of our decision to spend the winter in Jamaica, especially when we watched the weather report on TV at nights—never-ending pictures of the worst winter in the history of southwestern Ontario. Pat confirmed this on our telephone calls and congratulated us on our decision to get away from it.

In the middle of February, our son Carl, now living and working in Kenya, told us that he was coming to Jamaica to celebrate his birthday with his twin Judy, whom he would bring over from Canada. Fay and Dave were most excited about this and we planned an enormous birthday party for our twins. Fay set it all up with a host of caterers, jerk specialists and pumpkin soup makers. The 17th of February came and the folks arrived from near and far. They included my classmate Georgie Monroe, his ex-wife Pat, and cousins Audrey and Rosie from Kingston. Roger picked up Carl at Montego Bay and waited for Judy. Her multiple-transfer flight got screwed up and she landed up in Chicago in a snow storm so she arrived in Mo-Bay a few hours later. Roger had returned to pick her up. By the time she arrived the party was in full swing and the food nearly all devoured but we waited for her for the cutting of the traditional happy birthday cake. What a glorious day for Margaret and me to have our family with us in my homeland with many extended family and good friends.

The following day Roger took us all on an island tour. Jamaica is such a small island it can be completely traversed in a day. We decided to take it easy and broke our journey in Port Antonio in the home of my schoolmate Georgie Monroe. Georgie was in my class at Wolmer's and he often visited our home as he was far away from Port Antonio and boarding in Kingston. It was evident that Georgie's interest was in the sea and sea faring. One weekend, he took me out in his small motor boat to some small islands in Kingston harbour. He stopped the engine and told me that this was a great place to swim so I jumped in. I was enjoying the warm calm water when I saw what I thought was the fin of a shark in the distance. I quickly called out to Georgie "Shark, shark!"

"Don't worry, Colin, him far away. I'll tell you when he come near."

I rapidly returned to the boat and jumped in while Georgie laughed. Over the years Georgie became a qualified sea pilot and the foremost pilot in that area of the Caribbean. He married Pat Preston, a young beauty whose attention I once sought unsuccessfully. They had three children but Georgie's wayward ways led to the dissolution of their marriage. Pat went to live in England with their children while Georgie continued his Caribbean sea piloting. Strangely, despite their divorce Georgie and Pat remain close friends and Pat comes annually to spend time with him and their children in Port Antonio. Roger took us all to Port Antonio where we spent a most enjoyable evening with the Monroes. We had a guided tour of Georgie's eight-bedroom mansion which he had painstakingly constructed over many years.

He also took us on a tour of the historic ancient part of the city of Port Antonio.

We visited Errol Flynn's marina. This swashbuckling movie actor discovered his hideaway on a small island in Port Antonio harbour. He anchored his yacht *Zacca* there and that is where he held his infamous weekend parties. Errol died but his wife, herself a former movie star, remained in Jamaica, undertaking a remarkable amount of philanthropic work to this day. Roger expertly guided us along the beautiful north coast road until we were back in the familiar territory of St Mary's. We made the mandatory stops at various renowned jerk chicken and jerk pork roadside stands. The food was usually accompanied by a unique cake-like bread called "festival". Roger washed all this down with bottles of Red Stripe Beer.

I thought of the rigid blood alcohol levels allowed in Canadian drivers which Robert surely exceeded but in fact it seemed to sharpen his driving judgement and reactions. Carl and Judy were most impressed by this trip and I was pleased to see them so happy in my homeland. Soon they returned to their homes in the UK and Canada and Marg and I settled into our pleasant days at Pilgrim's Lodge.

The next big affair was a celebration of my 84th birthday on the 26th of March 2014. In her usual hospitable and efficient style, Fay threw an enormous party for me at Pilgrim's Lodge. The usual extended family from Kingston was there as were a host of my neighbourhood friends. Soon we prepared to return to Canada, on March the 30th. I was overcome by the kindness and love shown to Margaret and me in Jamaica. It was a wonderful experience for me to re-acquaint myself with the food, beauty, language and never-ending problems of Jamaica.

Chapter Twenty-seven

BACK TO CANADA

Returning to Canada was a strange experience for me. It was re-introduction to life on another planet. There is so much difference in everyday living between the two countries. Patricia and Judy and Chris and her friend Andy welcomed us back to our retirement home apartment. The winter was in its last throes after one of the worst in history and we heard many stories about the hardships it had caused. We were welcomed with many surprises—a room full of balloons wishing me a happy 84th, a cake, a new reclining sofa set and a sumptuous meal.

The following day we had a summit meeting and Marg and I decided to accept Patricia's offer of moving in to her house. She would take the downstairs and allow us to use the entire upstairs. Her condo is in a semi-secluded secure area in the south of the city. We had visited her many times before, enjoying her hospitality. Chris and Andy had moved out of the downstairs apartment and were living in an uncomfortable, unsafe area of the city. Margaret and I once again prepared to move—for the last time, I swore. The entire gang helped us in this tiring task and soon we were settled into our new and hopefully final home.

Unfortunately one of Judy's health problems reoccurred. She has a rare complication of diabetes, a skin condition called necrobiosis lipoidica diabetorium. It causes degeneration of the collagen tissue with a granulomatous response in her right leg. It started many years ago in Kenya and was intensely treated by a number of specialists including many skin grafts by plastic surgeons. Although it left a disfiguring scar in her leg it had otherwise been quiescent for more than 20 years. But it flared up again in early 2014 when she was visiting Jamaica. We were most upset and Margaret thought it was an omen of the imminent loss of her leg. "Why should all this happen to her?" Margaret cried and prayed to her favorite saint, St Jude, he of the impossible. I undertook a series of dressings of her lesions. For awhile I thought that the treatment was succeeding—but it wasn't.

I insisted that she go to her family doctor for further care. She referred to a wound care specialist who quickly instituted a program in an attempt to heal the lesions and prevent any disastrous outcome. The program consisted of dressings in a wound care unit run by the Victoria Order of Nurses. These wonderful, expert, compassionate nurses undertook the ongoing care of her skin condition. I took her to the unit for her dressings three times a week for about 10 months. Her wounds are now completely healed. Margaret thanked St Jude and I am very grateful that we are in Canada enjoying the expert health care system. I support Judy fully as she has chosen to live by herself and not seek any gainful employment.

We wondered about this until one day she summoned us to a meeting and described in a vivid, emotional way a horrible event that had taken place when she was 16 years old. We were at the coast and the teenagers went for their usual parties at the tourist hotels. There Judy was accosted by a number of young white men, young non-uniformed members of the British Army. They plied her with drink, took her to a room and gang raped her. I remembered her acting strangely that weekend but she did not explain the reason. Now, 35 years later, she decided that she could no longer live with the memory and wanted to tell us about it. It is obvious to me that she suffers from post-traumatic stress disorder. This explains much of her strange, sometimes antisocial, aggressive non-responsive behaviour, which has disturbed us so much through the years. We all tried to support her and thanked her for eventually telling us about this terrible event. That seemed to help Judy a bit, but it increased my resolve to do my best in any way possible to try to help my beloved daughter to go through her healing process.

On my return to Canada, I tried my best to return to work. My previous clinic, Medpoint, welcomed me back but quickly outlined the new system under which they operated. It was a complete switch from a paper-based to a computer-operated record system. Being only semi-literate in computers I explained my situation to the powers that be. I was assured that there would be a full support system in place to help me to switch over, regardless of my level of computer proficiency. I was enlisted into the program and guided through it by a kind, fast-talking woman. I understood about 20 per cent of what she said but she gave me my exit exam which in an amazing example of sleight of hand I passed with droopy colours and was awarded my e-certificate. I tried my skills out for awhile but I was a complete failure.

I just could not convert my attitudes, thinking and practice in my medical consultation face to face to be replaced by a computer screen and keyboard. I am told that this is indeed the way to practise modern medicine. I do not believe it and still think that spending time speaking to the patient with appropriate eye contact and empathetic responses is much more rewarding for all concerned instead of looking at a computer screen, typing out all the facts, then prescribing, then dismissing the patient with minimal person-to-person contact. I am told that this is the future of medicine and indeed the government of Ontario has spent billions of dollars to switch over to this paperless (heartless) method of medical care. I left the clinic, a complete e-medicine failure and looked about for an alternative, mostly to meet my financial demands for the upkeep of my family's needs. In desperation, I phoned a walk-in clinic where I once worked and asked them if they had an opening for me in a non e-health setting. Fortunately, the clinic manager with whom I had worked previously assured me that they were still paper recording and indeed I was welcome to return. After the required re-registration I was given clinics on a regular basis.

I enjoy this return to my profession even though I have to see many adults also. I have quickly re-learned all the necessary adult medicine including the management of various stages of hypertension, dementia and endless back pains. New to my diagnostic ability and care were the seemingly endless cases of sexually transmitted diseases. I wondered why anyone undertook behaviour leading to such a disease any more. The common complaints of anxiety, depression and aggression were most disturbing to me. They manifest themselves in a variety of patients—young and old, rich and poor, and they all require expert help. Such help is often difficult to obtain quickly so in the interim I became a de facto support mechanism for these needy folk. I must admit that the most enjoyable part of my work in these walk-in clinics was pay day. Then I would collect an enormous amount of money, mostly in the thousands, even with the 30 per cent deduction by the clinic. I am ashamed of this because never before had I practised medicine for money. Even in the hey-day of my private practice in Nairobi I was unable to tell how much money I was making. I only knew it was enough to meet the needs of my family and all the other folk whom Margaret saw fit to help—school fees for staff, burial expenses, special needs for the poor, church dues, and so forth.

But I continue down the road, enjoying the work that I can still do and proud of the help that I can still provide to those who need it!

COLIN E. FORBES

THE END—FOR NOW

The happy ending.

CPSIA information can be obtained
at www.ICGtesting.com
Printed in the USA
LVOW05s0011080616
491562LV00014BA/37/P

9 781988 186849